I0103545

Board of State Prison Commissioners   Montana

Annual report of the Board of State Prison Commissioners of

the state of Montana

Board of State Prison Commissioners Montana

Annual report of the Board of State Prison Commissioners of the state of Montana

ISBN/EAN: 9783744789585

Printed in Europe, USA, Canada, Australia, Japan

Cover: Foto ©Andreas Hilbeck / pixelio.de

More available books at **www.hansebooks.com**

FIRST ANNUAL REPORT

B

Pri······s,

INDEPE······O.,

FIRST ANNUAL REPORT.

OFFICE BOARD OF STATE PRISON COMMISSIONERS, }
HELENA, MONTANA, December 1st, 1891. }

To His Excellency, Joseph K. Toole, Governor of Montana:

In conformity to the law and the statutes of the State of Montana, the Board of State Prison Commissioners submit this, their First Annual Report, showing their proceedings for the year ending December 1st, 1891.

During the year last past the duties of the several members of the board in their several departments has been such that it was impossible to give the time and attention to the inspection of the prison and prisoners that might be required by legislative authority.

What the board has failed to perform in that direction it believes it has met by prison regulations, which require from the contractors full and complete reports concerning the happening of any event in the prison.

The board has, in the absence of legislative license, assumed to control the management of the said prison at Deer Lodge, by framing and adopting rules for the governing of the contractors and employes, and for the government and discipline of the prisoners confined in the State Prison.

In view of the fact that the prison rules were not adopted until September 3, 1891, we find it impossible to obtain from the records complete tables for the entire fiscal year ending December 1st, 1891; therefore we have not deemed it advisable to make an extended report, and content ourselves with calling the attention of Your Excellency to the tables herein enclosed from A to F inclusive:

1. Table A shows the number of State prisoners confined in the State Prison on December 1, 1891, with tabular references thereto.

2. Table B shows the name of each prisoner who had been punished for violation of the prison rules during the fiscal year, the offense committed and the mode and extent of punishment.

3. Table C shows the names of all prisoners discharged from the prison for the fiscal year ending December 1, 1891.

4. Table D shows the amount of money belonging to the prisoners confined in the prison for the fiscal year ending December 1, 1891, with the amounts set opposite the name of each, showing a total of $1,503.21.

5. Table E shows a list of the prisoners treated by the prison physician for the month of November, 1891, with the list of their diseases and the nature of the treatment and result of such treatment.

RECAPITULATION.

Number in prison December 1, 1890		242
Discharged by expiration of sentence	90	
Discharged by pardon	5	
Discharged on writ habeas corpus	2	
Delivered to sheriffs for new trial	3	
Transferred to insane asylum	2	
Died	3	
Escaped and since recaptured	2	
Total released	—	107
		135

Number received from December 1, 1890, to December 1, 1891.. 173

Number in prison December 1, 1891................. 308

6. Table F shows expenses incurred by the Board of Prison Commissioners for the fiscal year ending December 1, 1891.

Respectfully submitted,

JOSEPH K. TOOLE,

Governor and President of the Board.

H. J. HASKELL,

Attorney General.

L. ROTWITT,

Secretary of State and Secretary of the Board.

Members of the Board of State Prison Commissioners.

TABLE

STATE PRISONERS CONFINED IN MONTANA STATE PENI

Name of Prisoner.	Nativity.	Age	Height, in Feet and Inches	Weight	Occupation.	Marriage State	County Convicted In.
Ah Tek	China	40	5. 2	120	Cook	S	Silver Bow
Ah Wing, 1	China	34	5.	110	Cook	S	Missoula
Ah Wing, 2	China	29	5. 5	125	Cook	S	Beaverhead
Ah Jim	China	35	5. 3	120	Laundryman	S	Lewis & Clarke
Anderson, Robert F.	Minnesota	30	5. 9	138	Druggist	S	" "
Anthony, David	New York	46	5. 7	170	Brickmaker	S	Cascade
Angel, Frederick	Ohio	18	5. 5¼	130	Engineer	S	Lewis & Clarke
Allen, William H.	Washtanaw, Mich.	40	5. 8¼	155	Teamster	M	Deer Lodge
Blair, Jacob	Hamburg, N. J.	23	5. 6¼	155	Butcher	S	Custer
Brown, Martin	Galway, Ireland	20	6.	170	Plumber	S	Lewis & Clarke
Bennett, Rose	Salem, Ill	21	5. 4½	165	Demi Monde	S	Deer Lodge
Boyer, Alfred	Marysville, Canada	31	5. 6½	125	Laborer	W	"
Burton, Warren	Wheeling, Va	24	5. 3	128	Cowboy	S	Yellowstone
Brown, Edward	Bangor, Me	38	5. 0	175	Laborer	S	Cascade
Bond, John M	Wheeling, Va	30	5. 4¼	135	Bricklayer	S	Lewis & Clarke
Brazier, Albert E.	Nashville, Tenn	23	5. 7	130	Laborer	S	Custer
Bennington, Richard.	Alexandria, Mo	31	5. 9	170	Railroader	S	Park
Bray, John	Elmira, N. Y	30	5. 7¾	160	Horseman	S	Deer Lodge
Baker, James	Missouri	35	5. 7½	158	Blacksmith	S	Lewis & Clarke
Bailey, Carl	Massachusetts	38	5. [illegible]	160	Cook	S	" "
Burnes, Thomas	Detroit, Mich	29	5. 6½	139	Cook	S	Cascade
Brown, John H	New York	42	5. 5	135	Laborer	W	Lewis & Clarke
Brady, Florence	Princeton, Wis	20	5. 5	145	Dressmaker	M	Silver Bow
Brady, Frank	Springfield, Ill	28	5. 6¾	171	Miner	M	Silver Bow
Briyd, Frank	St. Louis, Mo	35	5. 0	180	Salesman	M	Gallatin
Bright, George	Ohio	15	6 1¼	150	Farmer	S	Dawson
Bryant, Charles W	Cincinnati, Ohio	31	5. 2½	120	Cook	S	Cascade
Burt, Harry	Schenectady, N. Y	24	5. 6¼	136	Laborer	S	Lewis & Clarke
Breen, Jean	Marseillies, France	27	5. 3¾	121	"	S	Cascade
Bickell, William	HaKah, Minn	23	5. 0	150	Cabinet Maker	S	"
Burns, William	Rostville, Iowa	22	5. 7¾	145	Laborer	S	Yellowstone
Cambell, Joseph	Philadelphia, Penn	20	5. 7¼	140	Rivet Maker	S	Chotean
Cambell, James	Winchester, Ind	30	5. 10	105	Stock Raiser	S	Deer Lodge
Cannon, Thomas	Sussex, England	42	5. 11	161	Jeweller	S	Lewis & Clarke
Clayton, Charles	New Orleans, La	40	5. 6½	170	Farmer	W	Silver Bow
Connolly, Michael	New York, N. Y	22	5. 7	145	Laborer	S	Beaverhead
Cavanaugh, Daniel	Dablin, Ireland	30	5. 5¾	133	Fireman	S	Missoula
Canning, John	Birmingham, Ala	20	5. 7	150	Miner	S	Silver Bow
Chandonnet, Napol'n.	Three Rivers, Can.	38	5. 8	170	Waiter	S	"
Chambers, Edward S.	Minneapolis, Minn	20	5. 8¼	165	Tinner	S	Lewis & Clarke
Corbin, Edward M	Campbell, N. Y	47	5. 9¼	105	Laborer	M	Cascade
Cummings, John S.	Springfield, Ill	32	5. 8½	136	Cow Boy	S	Yellowstone
Callahan, John	Cork, Ireland	33	5. 5¼	130	Laborer	S	Deer Lodge
Calvin, Thos. J	Carthage, Mo	21	5. 5	155	Miner	S	Missoula
Collins, Thomas	Waterford, Ireland	27	5. 7¼	165	Laborer	S	Silver Bow
Clark, Henry	Stevania, Norway	24	5. 5	125	Machinist	S	Lewis & Clarke
Clark, Myrtle	Davenport, Iowa	20	5. 5	140	Demi Monde	S	" "
Curns, Charles	San Francisco, Cal	24	6. 1¼	160	Railroader	S	Beaverhead
Click, Henry	Salem, Mo	23	5. 8¾	100	Farmer	S	Choteau
Cutler, Arthur	Port Huron, Mich	22	5. 4½	135	Rancher	S	Custer
Carter, George	Philadelphia, Pa	26	5. 2½	129	Laborer	S	Park
Conning, Bert.	Newburg, N. Y	32	5. 5	138	Cigar Maker	S	Silver Bow
Conley, John	Oswego, N. Y	32	5. 6¾	160	Bricklayer	S	Park
Carton, Matthew	New York, N. Y	35	5. 9½	160	Shoemaker	S	"
Donnegan, Charles	Maryland	35	5. 2½	120	Hostler	S	Silver Bow
Doyle, Douglas	Michigan	26	5. 7½	137	Miner	S	Custer
Daily, John	Boston, Mass	27	5. 7	145	Cook	S	Deer Lodge

A.

TENTIARY, DEER LODGE, MONTANA, DECEMBER 1st, 1891.

Crime.	Term.	Date of Sentence.	Expiration of Sentence Without Good Time	Expiration of Sentence With Good Time Full	Number of Previous Convictions	Indictment or Information.
Assault to kill	5 years	Mar. 8, 1890	Mar. 8, 1895	Dec. 8, 1893	None	Indictment
Murder, 2d degree	Life	Nov. 25, 1882			"	"
" "	Life	Oct. 17, 1889			"	"
Manslaughter	8 years	Mar. 11, 1890	Mar. 11, 1898	June 11, 1895	"	"
Forgery	3 "	Sept. 24, 1890	Sept. 24, 1893	Mar. 24, 1893	"	"
Grand larceny	2 "	Feb. 9, 1891	Feb. 9, 1893	Nov. 9, 1892	"	"
Forgery	1 "	Sept. 5, 1891	Sept. 5, 1892	Aug. 5, 1892	"	Information
Bigamy	1 "	Oct. 24, 1891	Oct. 24, 1892	Sept. 24, 1892	"	Indictment
Burglary	2 "	May 21, 1890	May 21, 1892	Feb. 21, 1892	"	"
"	12 "	Nov. 14, 1888	Nov. 14, 1900	Feb. 14, 1899	"	"
Murder, 2d degree	13 "	May 4, 1889	May 4, 1901	Aug. 4, 1896	"	"
" "	Life	May 25, 1885			"	"
Grand larceny	15 years	May 27, 1887	May 27, 1902	Feb. 27, 1896	"	"
Assault to rape	5 "	Oct. 27, 1890	Oct. 27, 1895	July 27, 1894	"	"
Assault to rob	8 "	Dec. 22, 1888	Dec. 22, 1896	Mar. 22, 1894	"	"
Murder	10 "	Feb. 1, 1890	Feb. 1, 1900	May 1, 1896	"	"
Burglary	3 "	Oct. 25, 1890	Oct. 25, 1893	Apr. 25, 1893	"	"
Manslaughter	7½ "	Nov. 15, 1890	May 15, 1898	Nov. 15, 1895	"	"
At. to commit burglary	2 "	Nov. 8, 1890	Nov. 8, 1892	Aug. 8, 1892	"	"
Grand larceny	4 "	Sept. 24, 1890	Sept. 24, 1894	Nov. 24, 1893	"	"
" "	1½ "	Feb. 9, 1891	Aug. 9, 1892	June 9, 1892	"	"
Burglary	1 "	Mar. 11, 1891	Mar. 11, 1892	Feb. 11, 1892	"	"
Grand larceny	1 "	June 29, 1891	June 29, 1892	May 29, 1892	"	"
Grand larceny	3 "	June 29, 1891	June 29, 1891	Dec. 29, 1893	"	"
Obtaining money on false pretense	2 "	Apr. 13, 1891	Apr. 13, 1893	Jan. 13, 1893	"	"
Burglary	2 "	May 6, 1891	May 6, 1893	Feb. 6, 1893	"	Information
Obtaining money on false pretense	1½ "	June 26, 1891	Dec. 26, 1892	Oct. 26, 1892	"	"
Burglary	2½ "	June 6, 1891	Dec. 6, 1893	July 21, 1893	"	"
Grand larceny	1 "	June 20, 1891	June 20, 1892	May 20, 1892	"	"
" "	2 "	Sept. 25, 1891	Sept. 25, 1893	June 25, 1893	"	"
" "	2 "	Nov. 3, 1891	Nov. 3, 1893	Aug. 3, 1893	"	"
Murder 2d degree	Life	Apr. 20, 1879			"	Indictment
Assault to murder	5 years	May 4, 1889	May 4, 1894	Feb. 4, 1893	"	"
Forgery	5 "	Mar. 11, 1890	Mar. 11, 1895	Dec. 11, 1893	"	"
Murder 2d degree	15 "	June 15, 1888	June 15, 1903	Mar. 15, 1897	"	"
" "	Life	June 15, 1881			"	"
" "		June 28, 1881			"	"
Burglarly	2 years	Sept. 22, 1890	Sept. 22, 1892	June 22, 1892	"	"
Infamous crime	5 "	June 14, 1890	June 14, 1895	Mar. 14, 1891	"	"
Grand larceny	1½ "	Oct. 3, 1890	Apr. 3, 1892	Feb. 3, 1892	"	"
Receiving stolen property	2 "	Feb. 9, 1891	Feb. 9, 1893	Nov. 9, 1892	"	"
Burglary	3 "	Feb. 20, 1891	Feb. 20, 1894	Aug. 20, 1893	"	"
Grand larceny	1 yr, 5m.	Apr. 1, 1891	Dec. 1, 1892	Sept. 21, 1892	"	Information
Murder 2d degree	10 years	July 13, 1891	July 13, 1901	Oct. 13, 1897	"	No record
Burglary	3 "	Nov. 16, 1891	Nov. 16, 1894	May 16, 1893	"	Information
Robbery	10 "	Nov. 5, 1891	Nov. 5, 1901	Aug. 5, 1893	"	Information
Grand larceny	1 "	Nov. 21, 1891	Nov. 21, 1892	Oct. 21, 1892	"	"
{ Burglary	3yr. 3m.	Mar. 11, 1891	June 11, 1891	Jan. 27, 1895	"	Indictment
{ Breaking jail	2 years					
Grand larceny	1½ "	Feb. 14, 1891	Aug. 14, 1892	June 14, 1892	"	"
" "	1 "	Mar. 9, 1891	Mar. 9, 1892	Feb. 9, 1892	"	"
Burglary	2 "	June 13, 1891	June 13, 1893	Mar. 13, 1893	"	"
Forgery	2 "	June 20, 1891	June 20, 1893	Mar. 20, 1893	"	No record
Burglary	3 "	July 9, 1891	July 9, 1894	Jan. 9, 1894	"	Information
{ Assaulting jailer	2 "	Nov. 2, 1891	Nov. 2, 1896	Aug. 2, 1895	"	"
{ Breaking jail	3 "					
Grand larceny	1 "	Oct. 10, 1891	Oct. 10, 1892	Sept. 10, 1892	"	No record
" "	7 "	May 14, 1887	May 14, 1891	Feb. 14, 1892	"	Indictment
Burglary	2 "	Sept. 17, 1890	Sept. 17, 1892	June 17, 1892	"	"

TABLE A—

Name of Prisoner.	Nativity.	Age	Height, in Feet and Inches	Weight	Occupation.	Marriage State…	County Convicted In.
Dearborn, Wm. A.	New York, N. Y.	35	5. 10¾	140	Civil Engineer	S	Lewis & Clarke
Durbin, William.	Shelbyville, Ind	31	5. 10	171	Laborer	S	Fergus
Duffy, Charles	Pittsburgh, Pa	26	6.	150	Cook	S	Silver Bow
Dolan, James	Milwaukee, Wis	22	5. 7¼	140	Plumber	S	"
Devine, Charles	Chicago, Ill	22	5. 4¾	130	Waiter	S	Lewis & Clarke
Davis, William	Glenwood, Iowa	42	5. 5	130	Laborer	S	Cascade
Dunn, Thomas	Pendleton, Oregon	36	5. 11	165	"	S	Fergus
Drew George	Canton, N. Y	40	5. 4¾	147	Cook	S	Cascade
Evans, Frank L.	San Francisco, Cal	20	5. 10	160	Plumber	S	Beaverhead
Edmonsen, Henry	Rochester, Mo.	30	5. 5¼	145	Laborer	S	Lewis & Clarke
Easton, William	Milwaukee, Wis	39	5. 8	165	Painter	S	" "
Estes, Mary	Ireland	45	5. 5	145	Laborer	M	Custer
Evans, John	England	50	5. 1	118	Miner	M	Lewis & Clarke
Evans, James	Owasson, Mich	24	6. 2¼	200	Horse Thief	S	Cascade
Ellis, Bert	Harrisburg, Pa	32	6.	195	Miner	S	Meagher
Fitzgerald, Michael	St. Joe, Mo	28	5. 7¼	150	Laborer	S	Choteau.
Frair, George	Watertown, N. Y	28	5. 3¼	155	"	S	Meagher
Fields, James	Troy, Mass	37	5. 4	145	"	S	Missoula
Finley, Larra	Minnesota	24	5. 7	175	Farmer	M	"
Furber, Juan	Bergen, Norway	21	5. 8	165	Baker	S	Park
Fischer, Clarence	Easton, Vt	35	5. 7¼	161	Laborer	S	Choteau.
Farrell, James.	Illinois	31	5. 8¼	160	Steam Fitter	S	Silver Bow
Flynn, William	New York, N. Y	47	5. 6	140	Laborer	S	Choteau
Frederickson, Wm. H	Milwaukee, Wis	37	5. 8¼	160	Blacksmith	M	Jefferson.
Fry, William	Muscatine, Iowa.	34	5. 5½	170	Miner	S	Deer Lodge
Foley, Michael	Waterford, Ireland	29	5. 7	130	Miner	S	Madison
Fish, James	Osceola, Iowa	24	5. 9¼	165	Butcher	S	Silver Bow
Fuller, Henry	Huntsville, Ala	34	5. 8¼	145	Cook	S	Park
Fitzpatrick, Michael	Iowa	34	5. 11	175	Railroader	M	Missoula
Fenton, William H.	St. John, N. B	20	5. 8	170	Brick Setter	S	Silver Bow
Furr, Sherman S.	Mooresville, N. C.	24	5. 6	150	Waiter	S	Lewis & Clarke
Fitzpatrick Patrick	Duluth, Minn	26	6. 1	180	R. R. Carpenter.	S	Missoula
Gibbs, James W	Hardin Co., Iowa	28	5. 8	150	Tel. Operator	W	Cascade
Grenier, Nazaire	Sorel, Canada	27	5. 6¼	180	Miner	S	Deer Lodge
Gordon, Charles	Dunnville, Canada	33	5. 0¼	160	Laborer	S	Choteau.
Grayson, Harry	Saratoga, N. Y	42	5. 7	150	Farmer	M	Yellowstone
Griffen, Andrew B.	Ohio	28	5. 6½	150	Railroader	S	Silver Bow
Gravel, Isaac	Canada	20	5. 4½	140	Laborer	S	Fergus
Grant, Archie	Minneapolis, Minn	28	5. 8¼	105	Stonecutter	S	Choteau.
Griffen, John W.	Baltic, Conn	43	5. 8½	165	"	M	Lewis & Clarke
Gore, Frederick J. T.	Brighton, England	32	5. 3	118	Newspaper Man.	M	" "
Guibbon, Henry	France	63	5. 6	135	Miner	M	Deer Lodge
Gouldon, John	Birmingham, Eng	40	5. 7	145	Laborer	S	Yellowstone
Galicher, Michael	Fortress Monroe, Va.	25	5. 8¾	160	Cigar Maker	S	"
Gelden, John C	Boston, Mass				Fireman	S	Cascade.
Gafney, Frank	Johnstown, Pa	27	5. 8	145	Cowboy.	S	Yellowstone.
Gendron, Antoine	Canada	46	5. 5¼	147	Shoemaker	M	Fergus
Grabhorne, Henry	Minnesota	20	5. 6½	150	Farmer.	S	Beaverhead
Gray, Frank	Buffalo, N. Y	32	5. 10	175	Stage Artist	S	Cascade
Gilbert, George	Chicago, Ill	21	5. 8	155	Laborer	S	Silver Bow
Gallus, William	Berlin, Germany	28	5. 6½	170	Farmer	S	Custer.
Hawkes, Daniel	Cork, Ireland	55	5. 6¼	155	"	M	Missoula
Hallenbeck, Ed'd L.	Chicago, Ill	30	5. 8½	140	Stenographer	W	Park
Hurst, Henry	Constantinople, Mich	26	5. 0¼	135	Miner.	S	Silver Bow
Havens, Merritt S.	Detroit, Mich	42	5. 6	140	Farmer	S	Cascade.
Hannaway, Charles B	Salem, Mass.	24	5. 3¾	141	Barber.	S	Fergus
Harris, William O.	Alexandria, Va	34	5. 8¾	155	Ore Sampler	M	Silver Bow
Howard, Charles P.	New York, N. Y	54	5. 11¼	160	Physician	W	Gallatin
Hoefke, Albert	Berlin, Germany	23	5. 8½	147	Cooper	S	Lewis & Clarke
Hagen, Michael	Chicago, Ill	40	5. 8¼	160	Laborer	S	Park
Hart, Daniel	Elk City, Idaho	31	5. 7½	160	Herder	M	Choteau.
Haggerty, John	St. Louis, Mo	33	5. 8¼	126	Laborer	S	Cascade.
Hennessy, John F	Watertown, Wis	34	5. 8¼	160	Miner	S	Beaverhead
Holland, William	Canada	39	5.	165	Laborer	S	Silver Bow
Hill, Peter	Toronto, Canada	45	5. 6¼	190	Miller.	S	Cascade
Hudson, William	Louisville, Ky	26	6.	160	Railroader	S	Silver Bow
Haynes, Charles	Detroit, Mich	26	5. 7	160	Cook	S	Gallatin

CONTINUED.

Crime.	Term.	Date of Sentence.	Expiration of Sentence without Good Time	Expiration of Sentence with Good Time Full	Number of Previous Convictions	Indictment or Information.
Grand larceny	1½ yrs	Apr. 9, 1891	Oct. 9, 1891	Aug. 9, 1892	None	Information
Assaulting jailer	3 "	Dec. 22, 1889	Dec. 22, 1892	June 22, 1892	"	Indictment
Burglary	2 "	Mar. 10, 1890	Mar. 10, 1892	Dec. 10, 1891	"	"
"	7 "	May 31, 1890	May 31, 1897	Feb. 28, 1895	"	"
Assault with deadly weapon	2 "	June 6, 1891	June 6, 1893	Mar. 6, 1893	"	Information
Grand larceny	2 "	Feb. 9, 1891	Feb. 9, 1893	Nov. 9, 1892	"	Indictment
Forgery	1½ "	May 11, 1891	Nov. 11, 1892	Sept. 11, 1892	"	"
Burglary	1 "	June 10, 1891	June 10, 1892	May 10, 1892	"	Information
"	7½ "	May 24, 1890	Nov. 24, 1897	May 24, 1895	"	Indictment
Grand larceny	14 "	Dec. 5, 1884	Dec. 5, 1898	Mar. 5, 1893	1	"
Forgery	5 "	Mar. 11, 1890	Mar. 11, 1895	Dec. 11, 1893	None	"
Rape	5 "	Mar. 10, 1891	Mar. 10, 1896	Dec. 10, 1894	"	"
Burglary	2 "	Sept. 23, 1891	Sept. 23, 1893	June 23, 1893	"	Information
Grand larceny	2 "	Mar. 14, 1891	Mar. 14, 1893	Dec. 14, 1892	"	Indictment
Assault with deadly weapon	1 "	Sept. 19, 1891	Sept. 19, 1892	Aug. 19, 1892	"	Information
Murder	20 "	Nov. 26, 1888	Nov. 26, 1908	Feb. 26, 1900	"	Indictment
Grand Larceny	7 "	Sept. 13, 1889	Sept. 13, 1890	June 13, 1891	"	"
Burglary	3 "	Dec. 7, 1889	Dec. 7, 1892	June 7, 1892	"	"
Manslaughter	10 "	Mar. 22, 1890	Mar. 22, 1900	June 22, 1896	"	"
Burglary	3 "	Jan. 25, 1890	Jan. 25, 1893	July 25, 1892	"	"
Grand larceny	3 "	Aug. 28, 1890	Aug. 28, 1893	Feb. 28, 1893	"	"
Burglary	7 "	May 31, 1890	May 31, 1897	Feb. 20, 1895	"	"
Grand larceny	5 "	Aug. 28, 1890	Aug. 28, 1895	May 28, 1894	3	"
Burglary	2 "	Jan. 12, 1891	Jan. 12, 1893	Oct. 12, 1892	None	"
Robbery	5 "	Oct. 18, 1890	Oct. 18, 1895	July 18, 1894	"	"
Murder 2d degree	Life	Mar. 20, 1879			"	"
Burglary	2 years	Sept. 22, 1890	Sept. 22, 1892	June 22, 1892	"	"
Forgery	2 "	Jan. 25, 1890	Jan. 25, 1892	Oct. 25, 1891	"	"
Grand larceny	1 "	Jan. 7, 1891	Jan. 7, 1892	Dec. 7, 1891	"	"
Burglary	1 "	Apr. 13, 1891	Apr. 13, 1892	Mar. 13, 1892	"	No record
Assault to murder	1 "	July 25, 1891	July 25, 1892	June 25, 1892	"	Information
Grand larceny	2 "	Oct. 27, 1891	Oct. 27, 1893	July 27, 1892	"	"
Perjury	7 "	May 15, 1890	May 15, 1897	Feb. 15, 1895	"	Indictment
Robbery	4½ "	May 11, 1887	Nov. 11, 1891	May 11, 1892	"	"
Murder	Life	Feb. 14, 1880			"	"
Forgery	3 years	Feb. 13, 1891	Feb. 13, 1893	Nov. 13, 1892	"	"
Grand larceny	1 "	Jan. 24, 1891	Jan. 24, 1892	Dec. 24, 1891	"	No record
Burglary	2yrs 9mo	May 15, 1891	Feb. 15, 1894	Sept. 9, 1893	"	Information
Grand larceny	1 year	Sept. 26, 1891	Sept. 26, 1892	Aug. 26, 1892	"	Indictment
"	2 "	July 10, 1891	July 10, 1893	Apr. 10, 1893	"	Information
Forgery	1 "	Sept. 26, 1891	Sept. 26, 1892	Aug. 26, 1892	"	"
Assault to murder	1 "	Mar. 14, 1891	Mar. 14, 1892	Feb. 14, 1892	"	Indictment
Manslaughter	10 "	May 27, 1891	May 27, 1901	Aug. 27, 1897	"	Information
Burglary	3 "	Nov. 3, 1891	Nov. 3, 1894	May 3, 1894	"	"
Murder 2d degree	18 "	Sept. 24, 1891	Sept. 24, 1909	Dec. 24, 1901	"	"
Assault to murder	4 "	Nov. 3, 1891	Nov. 3, 1895	Jan. 3, 1895	"	"
Murder 2d degree	18 "	Oct. 7, 1887	Oct. 7, 1905	Jan. 7, 1898	"	Indictment
"	Life	Oct. 13, 1887			"	"
Perjury	7 years	July 30, 1890	July 30, 1897	Apr. 30, 1895	"	"
Burglary	4 "	June 11, 1889	June 11, 1893	Aug. 11, 1892	"	"
Administering poison	4 "	Jan. 3, 1891	Jan. 3, 1895	Sept. 3, 1897	"	"
Murder 2d degree	10 "	Apr. 28, 1890	Apr. 28, 1900	July 28, 1896	"	"
Forgery	7 "	Sept. 22, 1887	Sept. 22, 1894	June 22, 1892	1	"
Robbery	10 "	Mar. 5, 1887	Mar. 5, 1897	June 5, 1893	None	"
Murder	18 "	June 10, 1888	June 10, 1906	Sept. 10, 1898	"	"
Assault to murder	10 "	Dec. 22, 1889	Dec. 22, 1899	Mar. 22, 1896	1	"
Burglary	3 "	Mar. 10, 1890	Mar. 10, 1893	Sept. 10, 1892	None	"
Forgery	5 "	Mar. 18, 1890	Mar. 18, 1895	Dec. 18, 1893	"	"
Burglary	2 "	May 23, 1891	May 23, 1893	Feb. 23, 1893	"	Information
Assault to kill	4 "	July 13, 1891	July 13, 1895	Sept. 13, 1894	"	"
Assault to rape	9 "	Sept. 26, 1891	Sept. 26, 1900	June 26, 1898	"	"
Robbery	2 "	June 18, 1891	June 18, 1893	Mar. 18, 1893	"	"
Assault to rape	1 "	Sept. 10, 1891	Sept. 10, 1892	Aug. 10, 1892	"	"
Burglary	6 "	Nov. 10, 1891	Nov. 10, 1897	Feb. 10, 1891	"	No record
Grand larceny	3 "	Mar. 14, 1891	Mar. 14, 1891	Sept. 14, 1893	"	Indictment
Burglary	2 "	Jan. 20, 1891	Jan. 20, 1893	Oct. 20, 1892	"	No record
Breaking jail	2 "	Sept. 13, 1890	Sept. 13, 1892	June 13, 1892	"	Indictment

TABLE A—

Name of Prisoner.	Nativity.	Age	Height in Feet and Inches	Weight	Occupation.	Marriage State	County Convicted In.
Harriman, Henry R..	Holland.	31	5. 6½	140	Harness Maker..	M	Cascade
Hill, Fred K. W.	Bazel, Switzerland..	26	5. 7¼	154	Painter	S	Lewis & Clarke
Harrington, George..	Detroit, Mich	19	5. 8½	130	Jailor	S	" "
Howard, Frank	Philadelphia, Pa	36	5. 7½	160	Laborer	S	Silver Bow
Irvine, Frank	" "	39	5. 4½	135	Lumberman	M	Park
Iliff, James W	Zanesville, Ohio	41	5. 4	160	Laborer	S	Cascade
Jackson, John	Wheeling, Va	35	5. 5½	155	Plasterer	S	Lewis & Clarke
Jessup, Alexander	North Carolina	25	5. 10	165	Farmer	S	Meagher
Jordan, Eugene	Plymouth, Mass	34	5.	125	Blacksmith	S	Dawson
Jaggers, Joseph	Galena, Ill	20	5. 11½	180	Miner	M	Beaverhead
Jones, Charles M	New York, N. Y	24	5. 7¼	150	Railroader	S	Custer
Jones, William W	Hudson, N. Y	23	5. 6	155	Laborer	S	Beaverhead
Johnson, Peter A	Sweden	27	5. 6½	160	Butcher	S	Deer Lodge
Jackson, Albert	Sherbrook, Canada	33	5. 10	163	Laborer	S	Lewis & Clarke
Jim Wah, Chung	Kong Chow, China	26	5. 8½	122	Cook	S	Silver Bow
James, John A.	Soo, Texas	35	5. 7¼	175	Cow Boy	S	Fergus
Jeffery, George W	Yonkers, N. Y	37	5. 5	140	" "	S	Yellowstone
Kasson, Walter F	Brooklyn, N. Y	26	5. 7¾	154	Tel. Operator	S	Cascade
Kelley, John A	Kansas City, Mo	30	5. 9	163	Bull Driver	S	Gallatin
Kelley, Joseph	Missouri	23	5. 3	135	Painter	S	Lewis & Clarke
Keefe, John	Glen Falls, N. Y	25	5. 9½	16[illegible]	Miner	S	Jefferson
Kelley, Thomas (1)	Montana	26	5. 10	161	Laborer	S	Gallatin
Kincaid, James	Ohio	37	5. 6½	150	"	M	Fergus
Kramer, Peter	New York, N. Y	39	5. 6½	160	Freighter	S	Choteau
Koken, Pierce	Birmingham, Pa	37	5. 6¾	125	Farmer	S	Deer Lodge
Kelley, Thomas (2)	St. Paul, Minn	24	5. 6	145	Butcher	S	Silver Bow
Kingsley, Albert	Canada	33	5. 9	161	Cow Boy	S	Deer Lodge
Lewis, Edwin T	Bushwick, N. Y	39	5. 5	130	Rancher	S	Custer
Lonick, Nathan L	Frankfort, Germany	46	5. 4	157	Physician	M	Lewis & Clarke
Lyle, John C	Springfield, Ill	20	5. 9	165	Clerk	S	Silver Bow
Leslie, James H	Maryland	36	6. 1	165	Miner	S	Lewis & Clarke
Langdon, Frank	Detroit, Mich	22	5. 7	145	Lithographer	S	Silver Bow
Lane, Charles	San Franciso, Cal	22	5. 5½	145	Jailor	S	Park
Leeper, Hugh	Springfield, Mo	37	5. 9½	165	Cow Boy	S	Custer
Lamb, John E	Columbus, Ohio	34	5. 8½	151	Railroader	M	Missoula
Lohmer, Charles	Westphalia, Germany	34	5. 6¾	136	Cabinet Maker	M	Cascade
Linnabarger, Wm. H	Perry, Mo	36	5. 6½	135	Laborer	M	Fergus
Lee, John	Finland	31	5. 10¾	180	Miner	M	Meagher
Lynch, Timothy	Diamond Lake, Ill	26	5. 8½	175	Laborer	S	Choteau
Lovegreen, Augustus	Chicago, Illinois	20	5. 9¾	160	"	S	Yellowstone
Leitch, Thomas	Lewiston, Idaho	23	6. ½	170	Cow Boy	S	Lewis & Clarke
Lumpp, Henry	Wurtemburg, Ger	44	5. 7	161	Brewer	M	Yellowstone
Linnemeyer, Frank	Minnesota	24	5. 11	165	Miller	S	Fergus
Manton, Dennis	Ireland	48	5. 5	152	Shoemaker	S	Deer Lodge
McDonald, Wm. R	Syracuse, N. Y	23	5. 7	175	Miner	S	Cascade
McKenzie, Edwin H.	Fort Worth, Texas	20	5. 10	152	Blacksmith	M	Lewis & Clarke
McGill, Charles	Sandusky, Ohio	30	5. 7½	145	Shirtmaker	S	Silver Bow
McGuire, Charles	Boston, Mass	27	5. 6	135	Shoemaker	S	Lewis & Clarke
Morgan, James	Rushville, Ohio	26	5. 6¼	130	Laborer	S	" "
McLaughlin, John	Elmira, N. Y	35	5. 7¼	175	Railroader	S	Silver Bow
Moran, James	Lawrence, Mass	25	5. 10½	170	Carpenter	S	Park
Montgomery, Richard	Mississippi	37	5. 3	130	Laborer	S	Lewis & Clarke
Mulligan, John	Ireland	31	5. 6½	140	Plasterer	S	" "
McNamara, Pat'k T.	Conshohocken, Pa	27	5. 6½	154	Stonemason	S	Choteau
Miller, William	Berlin, Prussia	20	5. 9	135	Iron Worker	S	Park
Meyer, Charles	Finland	65	5. 1¼	120	Jailor	W	Silver Bow
Matson, Henry	Illinois	22	5. 6	140	Laborer	S	Missoula
McGovern, James	Lafayette, Ind	28	5. 6½	146	Teamster	S	Lewis & Clarke
Mattler, Steven	Minnesota	25	5. 8	155	Bartender	S	Deer Lodge
McDonald, Louis H	Pittsburgh, Penn	45	5. 5	133	Carpenter	M	Choteau
McLung, William	" "	28	5. 4	145	Laborer	S	Silver Bow
Mosier, Urban	Germany	33	5. 10½	165	Miner	M	Park
Mahoney, John	New York, N. Y	23	5. 6¼	145	Railroader	S	Silver Bow
McCormick, Thomas	Shelbyville, Ky	35	5. 4¾	140	Laborer	S	Meagher
Manning, Henry	Castlebar, Ireland	39	5. 9	140	Musician	S	Silver Bow
Morgan, Edward	Whiteside, Ill	21	5. 9½	130	Railroader	S	Lewis & Clarke

CONTINUED.

Crime.	Term.	Date of Sentence.	Expiration of Sentence without Good Time	Expiration of Sentence with Good Time (Full)	Number of Previous Convictions	Indictment or Information.
Forgery	2 years	Oct. 27, 1890	Oct. 27, 1892	July 27, 1892	None	Indictment
Obtaining money on false pretenses	1½ "	Feb. 21, 1891	Aug. 21, 1892	June 21, 1892	"	"
Burglary	1 "	Feb. 21, 1891	Feb. 21, 1892	Jan. 21, 1892	"	"
"	1 "	July 28, 1891	July 28, 1892	June 28, 1892	"	No record
Forgery	2 "	July 20, 1891	July 20, 1893	Apr. 20, 1893	"	Information
"	3 "	Sept. 25, 1891	Sept. 25, 1894	Mar. 25, 1894	2	"
Robbery	10 "	Dec. 3, 1885	Dec. 3, 1895	Mar. 3, 1892	None	Indictment
} Robbery } Grand larceny	15 " 10 "	Sept. 10, 1884	Sept. 19, 1909	June 19, 1898	"	"
Crime against nature	15 "	Nov. 16, 1886	Nov. 16, 1901	Aug. 16, 1895	"	"
Grand larceny	5 "	Oct. 1, 1888	Oct. 1, 1893	July 1, 1892	"	"
Robbery	5 "	May 21, 1890	May 21, 1895	Feb. 21, 1894	"	"
Burglary	5 "	Oct. 8, 1889	Oct. 8, 1894	July 8, 1893	"	"
Murder	Life	Aug. 20, 1889			"	"
"	"	Apr. 5, 1890			"	"
Manslaughter	1 year	Apr. 16, 1891	Apr. 16, 1892	Mar. 16, 1892	"	No record
Murder 2d degree	22 "	May 15, 1891	May 15, 1913	Aug. 15, 1903	2	Indictment
Forgery	3 "	Oct. 22, 1891	Oct. 22, 1894	Apr. 22, 1894	None	"
Grand larceny	5 "	June 16, 1888	June 16, 1893	Mar. 16, 1892	"	"
Burglary	7 "	Apr. 21, 1887	Apr. 21, 1894	Jan. 21, 1892	"	"
"	4 "	Dec. 7, 1889	Dec. 7, 1893	Feb. 7, 1893	1	"
Robbery	7 "	Jan. 21, 1890	Jan. 21, 1897	Oct. 21, 1894	None	"
Attempt to rob	3 "	Dec. 26, 1889	Dec. 26, 1892	June 26, 1892	"	"
Assault with deadly weapon	2 "	Apr. 15, 1890	Apr. 15, 1892	Jan. 15, 1892	"	"
Grand larceny	1 "	Feb. 12, 1891	Feb. 12, 1892	Jan. 12, 1892	"	"
Burglary	2 "	June 6, 1891	June 6, 1893	Mar. 6, 1893	"	Information
"	1 "	July 28, 1891	July 28, 1892	June 28, 1892	"	No record
Grand larceny	5 "	Oct. 21, 1891	Oct. 21, 1896	July 21, 1895	"	Indictment
Assault to murder	3 "	May 17, 1890	May 17, 1893	Nov. 17, 1892	"	"
Forgery	4½ "	Apr. 5, 1890	Oct. 5, 1894	Sept. 20, 1893	"	"
Burglary	3 "	Mar. 10, 1890	Mar. 10, 1893	Sept. 10, 1892	"	"
Forgery	1 yr. 1 mo.	May 9, 1891	June 9, 1892	May 4, 1892	"	Information
Grand larceny	2 years	Jan. 10, 1891	Jan. 10, 1893	Oct. 10, 1892	"	No record
Burglary	5 "	June 13, 1891	June 13, 1896	Mar. 13, 1895	"	Information
Grand larceny	2 "	Mar. 7, 1891	Mar. 7, 1893	Dec. 7, 1892	"	Indictment
" "	1 "	June 15, 1891	June 15, 1892	May 15, 1892	"	"
" "	1¼ "	Sept. 30, 1891	Mar. 30, 1893	Jan. 30, 1893	"	Information
Assault to murder	6 "	Aug. 13, 1891	Aug. 13, 1897	Nov. 13, 1895	"	Indictment
Murder	Life	Nov. 23, 1891			"	Information
Grand larceny	6½ yrs	Sept. 26, 1891	Mar. 26, 1898	Mar. 26, 1896	"	"
" "	2 "	Nov. 3, 1891	Nov. 3, 1893	Aug. 3, 1893	"	Indictment
" "	5 "	Dec. 1, 1886	Dec. 1, 1891	Mar. 1, 1892	"	"
Murder 2d degree	15 "	Apr. 18, 1883	Apr. 18, 1898	Jan. 18, 1892	"	"
Grand larceny	2 "	Apr. 15, 1890	Apr. 15, 1892	Jan. 15, 1892	"	"
Murder 2d degree	10 "	Dec. 30, 1887	Dec. 30, 1897	Mar. 30, 1894	1	"
Grand larceny	8 "	Dec. 10, 1888	Dec. 10, 1896	Mar. 10, 1893	None	"
Forgery	5 "	Mar. 11, 1890	Mar. 11, 1895	Dec. 11, 1893	"	"
Robbery	7 "	May 24, 1890	May 24, 1897	Feb. 24, 1895	1	"
Burglary	7 "	Mar. 11, 1890	Mar. 11, 1897	Dec. 11, 1894	None	"
"	6 "	July 12, 1890	July 12, 1896	Oct. 12, 1894	"	"
Robbery	15 "	May 20, 1890	May 20, 1905	Feb. 20, 1898	"	"
Burglary	6 "	June 25, 1890	June 25, 1896	Sept. 25, 1894	"	"
Grand larceny	4 "	Mar. 11, 1890	Mar. 11, 1894	May 11, 1893	"	"
Burglary	5½ "	July 12, 1891	Jan. 12, 1897	July 12, 1894	"	"
Robbery	5 "	May 31, 1890	May 31, 1895	Feb. 31, 1894	"	"
Burglary	3 "	Oct. 25, 1890	Oct. 25, 1893	Apr. 25, 1893	"	"
"	1½ "	Nov. 6, 1890	May 6, 1892	Mar. 6, 1892	"	"
Assault to murder	3 "	June 30, 1890	June 30, 1893	Dec. 30, 1892	"	"
Forgery	3 "	Nov. 10, 1890	Nov. 10, 1893	May 10, 1893	"	"
Murder	Life	Oct. 18, 1890			"	"
Grand larceny	3 years	Feb. 13, 1891	Feb. 13, 1894	Aug. 3, 1893	"	No record
Murder	Life	Jan. 16, 1891	Jan. 16, 1893	Oct. 6, 1892	"	Indictment
Burglary	2 years	Jan. 20, 1891	Jan. 20, 1893	Oct. 20, 1892	"	No record
Assault to murder	8 "	May 6, 1891	May 6, 1899	Aug. 6, 1895	"	Indictment
Burglary	1½ "	Apr. 6, 1891	Oct. 6, 1892	Aug. 6, 1892	"	No record
"	1 "	July 9, 1891	July 9, 1892	June 9, 1892	"	Information

TABLE A—

Name of Prisoner.	Nativity.	Age	Height, in Feet and Inches	Weight	Occupation.	Marriage State	County Convicted in.
Murray, James	Canada	30	5. 5¾	150	Laborer	S	Silver Bow
Mason, Charles	Montreal, Canada	38	5. 8¼	145	Cook	S	Cascade
Morgan, Fred'k T.	New Jersey	25	5. 9	178	Laborer	S	Deer Lodge
McDonald, Pat'k P.	Montreal, Canada	25	5. 8¾	155	"	M	Choteau
McEntree, John	Ireland	25	5. 7	145	Cook	S	Missoula
McLin, James	Ottawa, Ill	47	5. 8¼	181	Carpenter	M	"
Monroe, Sidney	Buchanan, Mich	33	5. 6	155	Cow Boy	S	Yellowstone
Murray, Andrew	Glasgow, Scotland	21	5. 1	110	Butcher	S	Missoula
McDonald, Bryant	Kansas	31	5. 7¾	160	Farmer	S	Deer Lodge
McCarthy, John	Rochester, N. Y	24	5. 4	140	Plasterer	S	Lewis & Clarke
McMahon, Pat	Pittsburgh, Penn	30	5. 10½	175	Laborer	S	Jefferson
Miller, John	Baden, Germany	36	5. 8	155	Teamster	S	Yellowstone
McGlaughlin, Ter'nce	Rutland, Vt	33	5. 8¾	200	Engineer	M	Fergus
Nelson, James	Paris, Ky	63	5. 11	142	Horseman	W	Park
Nesh, William	Columbus, Ohio	63	5. 7	125	Blacksmith	W	Lewis & Clarke
Nieman, Edward	" "	21	5. 7¾	150	"	S	" "
O'Brien, James	Stockbridge, Mass	28	5. 7	151	Miner	S	Deer Lodge
Oleson, Charles	Sweden	21	5. 6¼	152	Cook	S	Lewis & Clarke
Overman, Charles	Columbus, Iowa	27	5. 6½	140	Porter	S	Missoula
Ormand, Thomas	New York, N. Y	22	5. 9	160	Laborer	S	Cascade
O'Neil, Frank	Chicago, Ill	23	5. 5¼	155	Iron Moulder	S	Deer Lodge
Oleson, Andrew H	Lanesboro, Minn	30	5. 6½	171	Carpenter	M	Lewis & Clarke
O'Leary, John	Harrisburg, Pa	30	5. 10½	168	Laborer	S	" "
O'Flinn, Thos. J	Ontario, Canada	22	5. 0¼	135	"	S	Cascade
Philip, John	Lewiston, Idaho	24	5. 0	145	Indian	S	Missoula
Page, William H	Williamsport, Pa	32	5. 5¼	157	Saloon Keeper	M	Yellowstone
Phelps, John	Springfield, Ill	22	5. 3¾	130	Cow Boy	S	Deer Lodge
Packard, John A	Troy, N. Y	37	5. 7	145	Canvasser	M	Park
Pearson, Bernard	Smaland, Sweden	38	5. 7½	149	Laborer	S	Missoula
Powess, Richard	Ireland	32	5. 11	185	Brick Maker	M	Silver Bow
Pendrey, Reuben	New York, N. Y	20	6. 1	185	Miner	S	Beaverhead
Quinn, Michael	Ireland	78	5. 7	147	Farmer	S	Jefferson
Reub, Albert F	Ross County, Ohio	24	5. 4	138	Steam Fitter	M	Lewis & Clarke
Ray, William	DesMoines, Iowa	17	5. 5	135	Confectioner	S	Beaverhead
Rowand, John A	Quebec, Canada	31	5. 8¾	145	Miner	W	Deer Lodge
Russell, Stuart	Indian Territory	27	5. 8¾	140	Cow Boy	S	Choteau
Rhodes, Willis	Pontiac, Ill	33	5. 6¼	173	Laborer	M	Meagher
Rossiter, William	Canada	20	5. 8	180	Laborer	S	Missoula
Riley, William J	Brooklyn, N. Y	18	5. 4	125	Machinist	S	Silver Bow
Randall, Albert E	Youngstown, O	28	5. 5	181	Shoemaker	M	Park
Rane, Frederick	Quebec, Canada	19	5. 4½	145	Laborer	S	Dawson
Root, William H	Madison, Wis	28	5. 10½	150	Railroader	M	Missoula
Raney, Curley	Texas	24	6.	160	Cowboy	S	Custer
Richards, Henry	Chicago, Ill	27	5. 10	150	Insurance Agent	M	Silver Bow
Rogers, Richard	E. Saginaw, Mich	17	5. 4½	125	Printer	S	Beaverhead }
Roach, William J	Oshkosh, Wis	21	5. 6	132	Bartender	S	Silver Bow
Ruf, Louis	Chicago, Ill	14	5. 2	130	Bootblack	S	Dawson
Ryan, James F	Dublin, Ireland	30	5. 1¾	125	Stenographer	S	Lewis & Clarke
Ryan, James	Philadelphia, Pa	37	5. 8½	155	Laborer	S	Silver Bow
Russell, Robert	East Indies	24	5. 6½	145	Herder	S	Choteau
Ryan, John	Pittsburgh, Pa	25	5. 3	132	Railroader	S	Silver Bow
Royels, Edward	Quincy, Ill	20	5. 7	150	Laborer	S	Meagher
Ryan, Daniel	Manchester, Eng	30	5. 3¼	180	Miner	M	Silver Bow
Saissom, Herman	Hamburg, Germany	28	5. 4¾	135	Farmer	S	Deer Lodge
Sterling, John	Pottstown, Pa	29	5. 5¼	145	Miner	S	Lewis & Clarke
Smith, Charles A	Chillicothe, O	33	5. 3½	100	Barber	S	Park
Smith, Walter	Canada	25	5. 4¼	135	Machinist	S	Lewis & Clarke
Smith, John (1)	St. Paul, Minn	20	5. 9	180	Plumber	S	" "
Smith, John (2)	Dublin, Ireland	23	6. 1¾	185	Laborer	S	Silver Bow
Smith, James (1)	Cleveland, Ohio	35	5. 4¾	150	Miner	S	Park
Smith, James (2)	Baltimore, Md	33	5. 5¼	135	Cook	S	Silver Bow
Smith, Albert	Richmond, Ky	24	5. 10¼	155	Miner	S	Missoula
Smith, Theodore	Freidheim, Ger	32	5. 11¾	175	"	S	Silver Bow
Smith, Charles	St. Louis, Mo	25	5. 4½	145	"	S	Park
Smith, Osceola	Richmond, Pa	23	5. 5	135	Barber	S	Yellowstone

CONTINUED.

Crime.	Term.	Date of Sentence.	Expiration of Sentence without Good Time	Expiration of Sentence with Good Time	Number of Previous Convictions	Indictment or Information.
Burglary	2 years	Apr. 20, 1801	Apr. 20, 1803	Jan. 20, 1893	None	Indictment...
Robbery	6 "	June 18, 1891	June 18, 1897	Sept. 18, 1895	"	"
Burgiary	1 "	Oct. 12, 1891	Oct. 12, 1892	Sept. 12, 1892	1	"
Grand larceny	1 "	June 1, 1891	June 1, 1892	May 1, 1892	None	"
" "	1 "	Oct. 6, 1891	Oct. 6, 1892	Sept. 6, 1892	"	Information..
Assault to murder	1 "	June 22, 1891	June 22, 1892	May 22, 1892	1	Indictment...
Burglary	5 "	Nov. 3, 1891	Nov. 3, 1896	Aug. 3, 1895	None	Information..
Forgery	1 "	Sept. 28, 1891	Sept. 28, 1892	Aug. 28, 1892	"	....
Manslaughter	2½ "	Oct. 24, 1891	Apr. 24, 1894	Dec. 9, 1893	"	Indictment...
Assault to kill	10 "	Nov. 22, 1888	Nov. 22, 1898	Feb. 22, 1895	"	"
Grand larceny	10 "	Mar. 10, 1889	Mar. 10, 1899	June 10, 1895	"	"
" "	10 "	May 27, 1887	May 27, 1897	Aug. 27, 1893	"	"
Burglary	2 "	Nov. 23, 1891	Nov. 23, 1893	Aug. 23, 1893	"	Infromation..
Robbery	5 "	Feb. 7, 1890	Feb. 7, 1895	Nov. 7, 1893	"	Indictment...
Forgery	1 "	Apr. 28, 1891	Apr. 28, 1892	Mar. 28, 1892	"	Information..
Burglary	2 "	Mar. 11, 1890	Mar. 11, 1892	Dec. 11, 1891	"	Indictment...
Murder 2d degree	15 "	June 3, 1891	June 3, 1901	Mar. 3, 1895	"	"
Robbery	15 "	Nov. 14, 1887	Nov. 14, 1902	Aug. 14, 1896	"	"
Murder 2d degree	12 "	Mar. 30, 1889	Mar. 30, 1901	June 30, 1896	"	"
Burglary	6 "	May 29, 1889	May 29, 1895	Aug. 29, 1893	"	"
"	1 "	Mar. 14, 1891	Mar. 14, 1892	Feb. 14, 1892	"	"
Forgery	1 "	Feb. 21, 1891	Feb. 21, 1892	Jan. 21, 1892	"	"
Burglary	1½ "	Apr. 8, 1891	Oct. 8, 1892	Aug. 8, 1892	"	Inforamtion..
Robbery	5 "	June 8, 1891	June 8, 1896	Mar. 8, 1895	"	Indictment...
Murder	Life	Mar. 25, 1890			"	"
Conducting fraudulent game of chance	1 year	Feb. 21, 1891	Feb. 21, 1892	Jan. 21, 1892	"	"
Perjury	1 "	Mar. 17, 1891	Mar. 17, 1892	Feb. 17, 1892	"	"
Assault to murder	4 "	July 13, 1891	July 13, 1895	Sept. 13, 1894	"	Information..
Grand larceny	1 "	July 8, 1891	July 8, 1892	June 8, 1892	"	"
Burglary	7 "	May 16, 1890	May 16, 1897	Feb. 16, 1895	"	Indictment...
Grand larceny	7 "	Oct. 1, 1888	Oct. 1, 1895	July 1, 1893	"	"
Assault to kill	1 "	July 11, 1891	July 11, 1892	June 11, 1891	"	"
" "	10 "	Dec. 4, 1886	Dec. 4, 1896	Mar. 4, 1893	"	"
Burglary	2 "	May 24, 1890	May 24, 1892	Feb. 21, 1892	"	"
Murder 2d degree	Life	May 2, 1888			"	"
Grand larceny	5 years	May 10, 1889	May 10, 1894	Feb. 10, 1893	"	"
Murder	10 "	Apr. 10, 1886	Apr. 10, 1896	July 10, 1892	"	"
Assault with deadly weapon	2 years	Oct. 16, 1890	Oct. 16, 1892	July 16, 1892	"	"
Voluntary manslaught'r	18 "	Oct. 23, 1885	Oct. 23, 1903	Jan. 23, 1896	"	"
Robbery	5 "	Feb. 7, 1890	Feb. 7, 1895	Nov. 7, 1893	"	"
Perjury	1 "	Feb. 9, 1891	Feb. 9, 1892	Jan. 9, 1892	"	"
Grand larceny	2 "	Apr. 9, 1891	Apr. 9, 1893	Jan. 9, 1893	"	"
Rape	5 "	Mar. 7, 1891	Mar. 7, 1896	Dec. 7, 1894	"	"
Grand larceny	1 "	Apr. 22, 1891	Apr. 22, 1892	Mar. 22, 1892	"	No record ...
Burglary	2yr 3mo	Mar. 11, 1891	June 11, 1894	Jan. 14, 1894	"	Indictment...
Breaking jail	1 year				"	
Robbery	6 years	June 27, 1891	June 27, 1897	Sept. 27, 1895	"	No record....
Burglary	1 "	May 7, 1891	May 7, 1892	Apr. 7, 1892	"	Information....
Forgery	5 "	June 20, 1891	June 20, 1896	Mar. 20, 1895	"	"
Forgery	1 "	July 13, 1891	July 13, 1892	June 13, 1892	"	No record...
Grand larceny	6½ "	Sept. 20, 1891	Mar. 20, 1898	Mar. 20, 1896	None	Information...
Burglary	1 "	Aug. 15, 1891	Aug. 15, 1892	July 15, 1892	"	No record...
Grand larceny	3 "	Sept. 19, 1891	Sept. 19, 1894	Mar. 19, 1894	"	Information...
Burglary	3 "	Nov. 20, 1891	Nov. 20, 1894	May 20, 1894	"	Indictment...
Attempt to murder	7½ "	Dec. 30, 1887	June 30, 1895	Dec. 30, 1892	"	"
Involunt'y manslaught'r	5 "	Jan. 5, 1889	Jan. 5, 1894	Oct. 5, 1892	"	"
Assault to murder	11 "	May 1, 1890	May 1, 1901	Feb. 1, 1897	"	"
Burglary	5 "	Nov. 14, 1888	Nov. 14, 1893	Aug. 14, 1892	"	"
"	4 "	July 12, 1890	July 12, 1894	Sept. 12, 1893	"	"
"	1 "	July 9, 1891	July 9, 1892	June 9, 1892	"	No record....
"	3 "	July 9, 1891	July 9, 1894	Jan. 1894	"	Information...
"	1 "	Oct. 28, 1891	Oct. 28, 1892	Sept. 28, 1892	"	No record....
Murder 2d degree	10 "	July 13, 1891	July 13, 1901	Oct. 13, 1897	"	Information...
Burglary	4 "	July 18, 1891	July 18, 1895	Sept. 18, 1894	"	No record....
"	2 "	Nov. 2, 1891	Nov. 2, 1893	Aug. 2, 1893	"	Information..
"	1 "	Nov. 3, 1891	Nov. 3, 1892	Oct. 3, 1892	"	

TABLE A—

Name of Prisoner.	Nativity.	Age	Height, in Feet and Inches	Weight	Occupation.	Marriage State	County Convicted in.
Shank, Lewis	Three Rivers, Mich.	30	5. 7¼	145	Engineer	S	Silver Bow
Street, John S	Gallopolis, Ohio	28	5. 7½	162	Laborer	S	Custer
Straight, Henry W	New York, N Y	17	5. 6½	150	"	S	Silver Bow
Stuart, Jessie	Duckport, Ky	19	5. 2½	125	Demi Monde	M	Deer Lodge
Schultz, Gustave	Prussia, Germany	27	5. 5¾	165	Farmer	S	Gallatin
Sullivan, John	Ireland	25	5. 7	150	Laborer	S	Silver Bow
Sullivan, Edward	Waterford, Ireland	42	5. 6	165	"	S	"
Salmon, John	New York, N Y	44	5. 7	125	Miner	S	"
Slussen, Andrew	Chicago, Ill	17	6. 1	177	Farmer	S	Park
Sheldon, William H	Athlone, Ireland	42	5. 5⅛	135	Bartender	W	Lewis & Clarke
Scheel, John R	Morgantown, W. Va.	37	5. ¼	150	Laborer	S	Choteau
Sims, Thomas	Austin, Tex	26	5. 7¾	143	"	S	Silver Bow
Sheffelberger, Chas. D	Lynchburg, Va	20	5. 9	180	Railroader.	S	Missoula
Swanson, Andrew	Christiana, Norway	48	5. 4	123	Painter	W	"
Schroeder, Frederick.	Cassel, Germany	37	5. 3¼	135	Laborer	S	Silver Bow
Stickney, Bert	Allegon, Mich.	17	5. 5	120	"	S	Custer
Shedd, Lester	Columbus, Ohio	24	5. 6	127	Clerk	S	Lewis & Clarke
Strider, George	Ohio	33	5. 8¾	150	Hostler	S	Gallatin
Stevens, Edward	Detroit, Mich	20	5. 7½	135	Teamster	S	Park
Steinhoff, Albert	Oxford, Canada	32	5. 6	150	Artist	S	Lewis & Clarke
Shatto, George	Tamerth, N. Y	19	5. 8	155	Herder	S	Yellowstone
Schneider, John	Herrington, Ger.	27	5. 5	150	Farmer	S	Fergus
Troudelle, Peter	Montreal, Canada	51	5. 4½	150	Laborer	M	Silver Bow
Teichert, Carl	Germany	34	5. 7½	145	Musician	M	Lewis & Clarke
Taylor, John H	Yonkers, N. Y	27	5. 8	140	Lumberman	S	Park
Titus, Daniel	Atlantic Ocean	49	5. 7¼	161	Machinist	S	Custer
Trushell, Frank	Warren, Pa	33	5. 6⅛	160	Laborer	S	Silver Bow
Thomas, Howell	Salt Lake, Utah	29	5. 5¼	155	Farmer	S	"
Thomas, Charles	Sealezer, Germany	36	5. 5½	125	Bricklayer	M	Lewis & Clarke
Thomas, William	Shreveport, La	21	5. 9	185	Dairyman	S	Custer
Teets, James A	Chicago, Ill	16	5. 4	140	Cook	S	Fergus
Thompson, George F	Covington, Ky	20	5. 10	150	Iron Worker	S	Jefferson
Thompson, William	Portland, Mo	40	5. 6¼	130	Baker	S	Cascade
Thurston, Henry	Louisville, Ky	33	5. 10	170	Laborer	S	Missoula
Tuney, Thomas	Indianapolis, Ind	31	5. 6½	130	"	S	Deer Lodge
Williams, Frank	Sacramento, Cal	21	5. 7¼	145	Iron Roller	S	Silver Bow
Williams, John	St. Louis, Mo	26	5. 8	170	Moulder	S	Lewis & Clarke
Williams, Henry	Illinois	31	5. 5¼	131	Cigar Maker	S	Silver Bow
Walker, B. Frank	Davis County, Mo	31	5. 5½	130	Tel. Operator	S	Jefferson
Walton, William	Wood County, Va	32	5. 7¼	142	Laborer	S	Deer Lodge
Warren, Alva J	Maryland	69	5. 7½	135	Carpenter	W	Madison
Whaley, Thomas	Santa Clara, Cal	29	5. 8½	165	Teamster	S	Choteau
Whaley, Daniel	Boston, Mass	27	5. 10¼	157	Painter	S	Lewis & Clarke
Woods, John	Mahomet, Ill	18	5. 7	141	Harness Maker	S	" "
Welch, Daniel J.	Syracuse, N. Y	22	5. 8	140	Railroader	S	Custer
Wyman, Frederick	Boston, Mass	29	5. 2¾	135	Herder	S	Silver Bow
Wilson, Thomas	Leadville, Col	24	5. 8	143	Printer	S	" "
Wright, Frank	Minneapolis, Minn	30	5. 6	155	Herder	S	Lewis & Clarke
Woodcock, James	Norridgewick, Me	25	5. 7¼	155	Butcher	S	Deer Lodge
Woods, Peter	Ireland	36	5. 5¼	165	Laborer	S	Jefferson
Wolf, Robert W	Elko, Nev	25	5. 7	155	"	S	Lewis & Clarke
You Loy	Hong Kong, China	26	5. 2	125	Laundryman	S	Silver Bow
Young, Elmer A	Knox, Me	21	5. 7	145	Laborer	S	Lewis & Clarke

CONCLUDED.

Crime.	Term.	Date of Sentence.	Expiration of Sentence without Good Time	Expiration of Sentence with Good Time	Number of Previous Convictions	Indictment or Information.
Robbery	10 years	Mar. 12, 1887	Mar. 12, 1897	June 12, 1893	None	Indictment...
Robbery	5 "	Sept. 12, 1888	Sept. 12, 1898	Dec. 12, 1894	"	" ....
Robbery	5 "	Sept. 12, 1888				
Grand larceny	4 "	May 11, 1889	May 11, 1893	July 11, 1892	"	"
Assault to murder	4 "	Apr. 26, 1889	Apr. 26, 1893	June 26, 1892	"	"
Burglary	3 "	Mar. 18, 1890	Mar. 18, 1893	Sept. 18, 1892	"	"
Robbery	8 "	Apr. 18, 1800	Apr. 18, 1898	July 18, 1895	"	"
Grand larceny	3 "	May 24, 1890	May 24, 1893	Nov. 24, 1892	"	"
Receiving stolen property	4 "	Oct. 27, 1890	Oct. 27, 1891	Dec. 27, 1893	"	"
Burglary	3 "	Oct. 25, 1890	Oct. 25, 1893	Apr. 25, 1893	"	"
Perjury	2 "	Nov. 10, 1890	Nov. 10, 1892	Aug. 10, 1892	"	"
Grand larceny	1 "	Sept. 22, 1891	Sept. 22, 1892	Aug. 22, 1892	"	" ....
" "	1½ "	Apr. 23, 1891	Oct. 23, 1892	Aug. 23, 1892	"	No record....
" "	2 "	Apr. 9, 1891	Apr. 9, 1893	Jan. 9, 1893	"	Indictment....
" "	1 "	July 8, 1891	July 8, 1892	June 8, 1892	"	Information..
Burglary	3 "	July 18, 1891	July 18, 1894	Jan. 18, 1894	"	No record....
Grand larceny	1 "	May 4, 1891	May 4, 1892	Apr. 4, 1892	"	" ....
Forgery	3 "	June 20, 1891	June 20, 1894	Dec. 20, 1893	"	Information..
Grand larceny	1 "	Oct. 24, 1891	Oct. 24, 1892	Sept. 24, 1892	"	" ....
Burglary	3 "	Nov. 10, 1891	Nov. 10, 1894	May 10, 1893	"	"
Forgery	1 "	Oct. 5, 1891	Oct. 5, 1892	Sept. 5, 1892	"	" ....
Grand larceny	2½ "	Oct. 22, 1891	Apr. 22, 1893	Dec. 7, 1893	"	Indictment....
Burglary	6 "	May 15, 1891	May 15, 1897	Aug. 15, 1895	"	" ....
Arson	3 "	Oct. 4, 1890	Oct. 4, 1893	Apr. 4, 1893	"	" ....
Assault to murder	1 "	Apr. 28, 1891	Apr. 28, 1892	Mar. 28, 1892	"	" ....
Burglary	4 "	June 25, 1890	June 25, 1894	Aug. 25, 1893	"	" ....
Murder 2d degree	30 "	June 1, 1882	June 1, 1912	Sept. 1, 1895	"	" ....
Grand larceny	4 "	May 10, 1889	May 10, 1893	July 10, 1892	"	" ....
Murder 2d degree	Life	Mar. 20, 1890				" ....
Assault to murder	3½ yrs.	Feb. 21, 1891	Aug. 21, 1894	Dec. 21, 1893	"	" ....
Grand larceny	2 years	Sept. 15, 1891	Sept. 15, 1893	June 15, 1893	"	Information..
Burglary	2 "	Sept. 20, 1890	Sept. 20, 1892	June 20, 1892	"	Indictment...
Rape	14 "	Jan. 7, 1891	Jan. 7, 1905	Apr. 7, 1900	"	" ....
Burglary	2 "	Feb. 9, 1891	Feb. 9, 1893	Nov. 9, 1892	"	" ....
Grand larceny	1½ "	Mar. 21, 1891	Sept. 21, 1892	July 21, 1892	"	" ....
Burglary	1 "	June 10, 1891	June 10, 1892	May 10, 1892	"	Information..
"	10 "	May 10, 1889	May 10, 1899	Aug. 10, 1895	"	Indictment...
"	3 "	July 12, 1890	July 12, 1893	Jan. 12, 1893	"	" ....
"	1½ "	July 8, 1891	Jan. 8, 1893	Nov. 8, 1892	"	No record....
Murder 2d degree	10 "	Mar. 8, 1889	Mar. 8, 1899	June 8, 1895	"	Indictment...
" "	Life	June 3, 1886				"
Manslaughter	10 years	Dec. 3, 1888	Dec. 3, 1898	Mar. 3, 1895	"	" ....
Burglary	1 "	Feb. 13, 1891	Feb. 13, 1892	Jan. 13, 1892	"	" ....
"	2 "	June 1, 1891	June 1, 1893	Mar. 1, 1893	"	Information..
"	1 "	Apr. 8, 1891	Apr. 8, 1892	Mar. 8, 1892	"	" ....
Robbery	5 "	May 21, 1890	May 21, 1895	Feb. 21, 1894	"	Indictment...
Grand larceny	1½ "	July 28, 1891	Jan. 28, 1893	Nov. 28, 1892	"	No record....
" "	1 "	July 8, 1891	July 8, 1892	June 8, 1892	"	" ....
Burglary	2 "	Oct. 2, 1891	Oct. 2, 1893	July 2, 1893	"	Information..
"	1 "	Oct. 21, 1891	Oct. 21, 1892	Sept. 21, 1892	"	Indictment...
Murder 2d degree	Life	Nov. 12, 1891				Information..
Forgery	2 years	Nov. 12, 1891	Nov. 12, 1893	Aug. 12, 1893	"	" ....
Burglary	4 "	Nov. 10, 1890	Nov. 10, 1894	Jan. 10, 1894	"	Indictment...
Forgery	4½ "	Sept. 24, 1890	Mar. 24, 1895	Mar. 9, 1894	"	" ....

TABLE B.

Showing Names of Prisoners Confined in Montana State Penitentiary, Deer Lodge, Montana, Who Have Been Punished for Violation of Rules From December 1, 1890, to December 1, 1891.

NAME.	Rule Violated	Date of Violation.	Extent of Violation.	Punishment—Mode and Extent.	Date of Punishment.
Ah Wing (No. 1)	No Record	Feb. 28, 1891	Disobedience and impudence	Dark cell; bread and water: 10 days	Feb. 28, 1891
Ah Jim	"	March 26, 1891	Disobedience	" 10 "	March 26, 1891
Anderson, Robert F.	"	May 22, 1891	Loud talking	" 10 "	May 22, 1891
Ah Jue	"	August 11, 1891	Trying to pass papers after hours	" 12 "	Aug. 11, 1891
Ah Tek	"	August 25, 1891	Disobedience to rules	" 26 "	Aug. 26, 1891
Baker, James	"	May 18, 1891	Secreting knife in cell	" 21 "	May 18, 1891
Boyer, Alfred	"	June 12, 1891	Refusing to obey orders	" 10 "	June 12, 1891
Bailey, Carl	"	June 28, 1891	Disorderly conduct	" 1 "	June 28, 1891
Brown, Martin	"	July 11, 1891	Fighting	" 10 "	July 11, 1891
Burns, Thomas	"	Oct. 19, 1891	Profane language	Escaped Oct.19, 1891	Oct. 19, 1891
Burns, Thomas	"	Oct. 24, 1891	Recaptured	In leg irons 10 days	Oct. 24, 1891
Bickell, William	No record	Nov. 16, 1891	Making noise	7 days	Nov. 16, 1891
Cavanaugh, Daniel	"	Jan. 11, 1891	Loud talking	7 "	Jan. 11, 1891
Cavanaugh, Daniel	"	Feb. 10, 1891	Fighting	15 "	Feb. 10, 1891
Cavanaugh, Daniel	"	March 7, 1891	Fighting	10 "	March 7, 1891
Chambers, Edward S	"	April 13, 1891	Stealing food from kitchen	10 "	April 13, 1891
Cavanaugh, Daniel	"	June 10, 1891	Disobeying rules	13 "	June 10, 1891
Chandonnet, Napoleon	"	June 16, 1891	Disorderly conduct	13 "	June 16, 1891
Chambers, Edward S	"	July 25, 1891	Disorderly conduct	8 "	July 25, 1891
Cavanaugh, Daniel	"	Sept. 17, 1891	Fighting	10 "	Sept. 17, 1891
Cutter, Arthur	57	Nov. 17, 1891	Using profane language	15 "	Nov. 17, 1891
Dearborn, Wm A	No record	July 29, 1891	Disorderly conduct	15 "	July 17, 1891
Ellis, Frank	52	Nov. 5, 1891	Loud talking	1 "	Nov. 5, 1891
Edmonson, Henry	No record	March 11, 1891	Loud talking	5 "	March 11, 1891
Fields, James	"	Feb. 3, 1891	Talking at table	10 "	Feb. 3, 1891
Fitzgerald, John P	"	Feb. 14, 1891	Fighting	10 "	Feb. 14, 1891
Fuller, Wm. H	"	March 11, 1891	Loud talking and laughter	10 "	March 11, 1891
Fry, William	"	April 23, 1891	Refusing to obey orders	7 "	April 23, 1891
Fitzgerald, Michael	"	April 29, 1891	Fighting	10 "	April 29, 1891
Fitzgerald, Michael	"	July 11, 1891	Fighting	8 "	July 11, 1891
Furr, Sherman S	"	Oct. 14, 1891	Fighting	5 "	Oct. 14, 1891
Fuller, Wm. H	"	Oct. 14, 1891	Fighting	Escaped Oct. 19, 1891; 6 days	Oct. 14, 1891
Goulden, John	52	June 13, 1891	Refusing to obey orders	Dark cell; bread and water; 10 days	June 13, 1891
Grayson, Isaac	57	Nov. 16, 1891	Making noise in cell	" 7 "	Nov. 16, 1891
Gravel, Harry	No record	Nov. 17, 1891	Profane language	" 10 "	Nov. 17, 1891
Howard, Charles P	"	Feb. 11, 1891	Disobeying rules	" 15 "	Feb. 11, 1891
Harry, Paul	"	Feb. 3, 1891	Fighting	" 9 "	Feb. 3, 1891

Name	Record	Date	Offense	Punishment	Days	Date
Harrington, George	No record.	March 11, 1891	Loud talking in cell	Dark cell; bread and water		March 11, 1891
Harry, Paul	"	Aug. 27, 1891	Disorderly conduct	"	10	Aug. 27, 1891
Haynes, Charles	"	Oct. 13, 1891	Loud talking	"	7	Oct. 13, 1891
Howard, Frank	"	Nov. 10, 1891	Refusing to obey orders	"	11	Nov. 10, 1891
Jones, William W	"	Dec. 7, 1891	Loud talking	"	5	Dec. 7, 1891
Jessup, Alexander	"	Jan. 4, 1891	Loud talking	"	5	Jan. 4, 1891
Jordan, Eugene	"	Jan. 8, 1891	Disobeying rules	"	11	Jan. 8, 1890
Kasson, Walter F	"	Dec. 7, 1891	Loud talking	"	10	Dec. 7, 1891
Kelley, Thomas (No. 1)	"	Feb. 3, 1891	Talking at table	"	8	Feb. 3, 1891
Kelley, Thomas (No. 1)	"	Aug. 19, 1891	Talking at table	"	6	Aug. 19, 1891
Leitch, Thomas	"	Jan. 12, 1892	Fighting	"	10	Jan. 12, 1891
Lannemeyer, Frank	"	May 4, 1891	Writing indecent letter	"	6	May 4, 1890
Lane, Charles	53	Oct. 13, 1891	Fighting	"	7	Oct. 13, 1891
Linnemeyer, Frank	No record	Nov. 10, 1891	Making noise	"	7	Nov. 16, 1891
McMahon, Patrick	"	Feb. 10, 1891	Fighting	"	6	Feb. 6, 1891
Matter, Steve	"	March 6, 1891	Loud talking	"	10	March 11, 1891
Miller, William	"	March 11, 1891	Loud talking	"	5	March 11, 1891
Matson, Henry	"	March 24, 1891	Disobedience	"	5	March 24, 1891
Mahoney, John	"	March 24, 1891	Passing note contrary to rules	"	7	March 24, 1891
McNamara, Patrick J	"	April 23, 1891	Disobeying orders	"	10	April 23, 1891
Moran, James	"	April 21, 1891	Disobeying orders	"	6	April 21, 1891
Matter, Steve	"	May 18, 1891	Secreting knife in cell	"	10	May 18, 1891
Mulligan, John	"	May 29, 1891	Disobedience	"	10	May 29, 1891
Matson, Henry	"	May 29, 1891	Disobedience	"	21	May 29, 1891
Matter, Steve	"	June 13, 1891	Refusing to obey orders	"	12	June 13, 1891
Moran, James	"	July 7, 1891	Refusing to obey orders	"	6	July 31, 1891
Murray, James	"	Oct. 31, 1891	Fighting	"	9	Oct. 27, 1891
O'Brien, James	"	Nov. 27, 1891	Fighting	"	7	Nov. 9, 1891
Rutledge, Joseph	"	Jan. 9, 1891	Fighting	"	20	Jan. 7, 1891
Ray, William	"	July 9, 1891	Disobeying rules	"	16	July 9, 1891
Rogers, Richard	"	March 5, 1891	Loud talking	"	10	March 5, 1891
Rutledge, Joseph	"	April 29, 1891	Disorderly conduct	"	10	April 29, 1891
Riley, William J	"	May 26, 1891	Laughing and loud talking	"	10	May 26, 1891
Rutledge, Joseph	"	June 12, 1891	Disobeying rules	"	14	June 12, 1891
Rutledge, Joseph	"	June 24, 1891	Disorderly conduct	"	14	June 24, 1891
Ryan, James F	"	July 25, 1891	Disorderly conduct	"	8	July 25, 1891
Rutledge, Joseph	"	Aug. 19, 1891	Talking at table	"	8	Aug. 19, 1891
Ryan, James F	57	Oct. 29, 1891	Profane language	"	17	Oct. 29, 1891
Ryan, John	No record	Nov. 1, 1891	Trying to escape by tunneling from cell	In irons Dark cell; bread and water;	7	Nov. 1, 1891
Smith, John (No. 1)	53	Nov. 10, 1891	Making noise	"	5	Nov. 16, 1891
Shiffelberger, Charles D	No record	Jan. 10, 1891	Attempting to pass note to prisoner	"	5	Jan. 10, 1891
Salmon, John	"	April 24, 1891	Loud talking	"	10	May 22, 1891
Salmon, John	"	May 23, 1891	Disobeying orders	"	22	April 24, 1891
Schultz, Gustave F	"	May 23, 1891	Violating rules	"	9	May 23, 1891
Smith, Charles A	"	Aug. 18, 1891	Cursing and fighting	"	5	Aug. 18, 1891
Shedd, Lester	"	Oct. 7, 1891	Fighting	"	5	Oct. 7, 1891
Smith, John (No. 2)	"	Nov. 10, 1891	Loud talking	"	8	Nov. 10, 1891
Schroeder, Frederick	"	Nov. 16, 1891	Violation of rules	"	7	Nov. 16, 1891
			Making noise			

TABLE B—CONCLUDED.

NAME.	Rule Violated.	Date of Violation.	Extent of Violation.	Punishment—Mode and Extent.	Date of Punishment.
Smith, John (No. 1)	50	Nov. 17, 1891	Visiting adjoining cell	Dark cell; bread and water; 10 days	Nov. 17, 1891
Stuart, Jessie	54	Nov. 10, 1891	Writing letter to prisoner	" 4 "	Nov. 19, 1891
Thompson, George F.	No record	April 29, 1891	Fighting	" 10 "	April 29, 1891
Tuney, Thomas	"	July 9, 1891	Fighting	" 7 "	July 9, 1891
Teets, James A.	52	Nov. 5, 1891	Loud talking	" 5 "	Nov. 5, 1891
Thurston, Harry	57	Nov. 17, 1891	Profane language	" 15 "	Nov. 17, 1891
Warren, Alva J.	No record	Dec. 5, 1890	Fighting	" 2 "	Dec. 5, 1890
Walton, William	"	Jan. 25, 1891	Fighting	" 5 "	Jan. 25, 1891
Williams, Frank	"	March 6, 1891	Loud talking	" 6 "	March 7, 1891
Walton, William	"	April 4, 1891	Disorderly conduct	" 10 "	April 4, 1891
Walton, William	"	April 30, 1891	Disorderly conduct	" 9 "	April 30, 1891
Walton, William	"	May 29, 1891	Disorderly conduct	" 10 "	May 29, 1891
Walton, William	"	July 9, 1891	Fighting	" 12 "	July 9, 1891
Walton, William	"	Sept. 23, 1891	Making knife	" 10 "	Sept. 23, 1891
You Loy	"	June 1, 1891			June 1, 1891

TABLE C.

Prisoners Discharged from Montana State Penitentiary, Deer Lodge, Montana, from December 1, 1890, to December 1, 1891.

NAME.	Nativity.	Age.	Occupation.	County Convicted In.	Crime.	Term of Sentence.	Date of Sentence.	Expiration of Sentence Without Good Time.	Expiration of Sentence With Full Good Time.	Good Time Allowed.
Wilson, Geo.	Kentucky	34	Machinist	Lewis and Clarke	Burglary	3 years	June 14, 1888	June 14, 1891	Dec. 14, 1890	6 months.
Wilson, A. B.	Missouri	29	Laborer	Chotcau	Assault to murder	1 year	Jan. 15, 1890	Jan. 15, 1891	Dec. 15, 1890	1 month.
Adamson, J. M.	Canada	26	Laborer	Chotcau	Grand larceny	1 year	Jan. 15, 1890	Jan. 15, 1891	Dec. 15, 1890	1 month.
Cunningham, C. J.	Wash. D. C.	29	Telegraph Operator	Jefferson	Embezzlement	1 year	Jan. 17, 1890	Jan. 17, 1891	Dec. 17, 1890	1 month.
Brown, Chas.	New Jersey	27	Butcher	Madison	Grand larceny	4 years	Oct. 27, 1887	Oct. 27, 1891	Dec. 27, 1890	10 months.
Manning, H.	Ireland	30	Musician	Dawson	Escaping jail	1 year	Jan. 3, 1890	Jan. 3, 1891	Dec. 3, 1890	1 month.
Mellen, H.	New York	39	Cook	Chotcau	Larceny as clerk	10 years	May 20, 1887	May 20, 1897	Aug. 20, 1893	Pardoned Jan. 4, 91.
Marlow, J.	Canada	37	Laborer	Missoula	Selling liquor to an Indian	30 days	Dec. 13, 1890	Jan. 12, 1891	Jan. 11, 1891	1 day.
Shiell, J.	Scotland	28	Laborer	Meagher	Forgery	1 year	Feb. 11, 1890	Feb. 11, 1891	Jan. 11, 1891	1 month.
Ahrenhold, H.	Germany	29	Laborer	Lewis and Clarke	Burglary	1 year	Nov. 17, 1889	Nov. 17, 1890	Jan. 17, 1891	10 months.
Peters, G.	New York	26	Clerk	Deer Lodge	Grand larceny	2 years	April 19, 1890	April 19, 1891	Jan. 19, 1891	3 months.
Terry, W.	Illinois	29	Laborer	Gallatin	Grand larceny	5 years	April 21, 1892	April 21, 1891	Jan. 21, 1891	1 yr. 3 mos.
Zminiski, J.	Germany	26	Farmer	Yellowstone	Grand larceny	2 years	April 25, 1889	April 25, 1891	Jan. 25, 1891	3 months.
Charlie, J. D.	China	30	Cook	Lewis and Clarke	Burglary	2 years	April 25, 1889	April 25, 1891	Jan. 25, 1891	3 months.
Dean, Thos.	Ireland	41	Laborer	Deer Lodge	Burglary	2 years	April 26, 1889	April 26, 1891	Jan. 26, 1891	3 months.
Maxwell, H.	Pennsylvania	25	Carpenter	Lewis and Clarke	Forgery	2 years	April 27, 1890	April 27, 1891	Jan. 27, 1891	3 months.
Walters, W. J.	Louisiana	35	Tinner	Missoula	Assault to kill	4 years	Nov. 26, 1887	Nov. 26, 1891	Jan. 26, 1891	9 mos 22 ds
Bingham, S.	New York	32	Teamster	Silver Bow	Forgery	1 year	Mar. 3, 1890	Mar. 3, 1891	Feb. 3, 1891	1 month.
Burton, A. C.	Kentucky	20	Laborer	Lewis and Clarke	Burglary	2 years	Dec. 7, 1889	Dec. 7, 1891	Sept. 7, 1891	Habeas Corpus Feb. 7, '91.
Smith, W. B.	Minnesota	41	Fireman	Custer	Grand larceny	5 years	May 14, 1887	May 14, 1892	Feb. 14, 1891	1 yr 3 mos.
Healey, C	Pennsylvania	43	Laborer	Yellowstone	Manslaughter	18 months	Oct. 19, 1889	April 19, 1891	Feb. 19, 1891	2 months.
Fletcher, N.	New York	33	Waiter	Yellowstone	Burglary	5 years	May 27, 1887	May 27, 1892	Feb. 27, 1891	1 yr 3 mos.
Lyons, P.	Massachusetts	26	Miner	Silver Bow	Manslaughter	1 year	Mar. 29, 1890	Mar. 29, 1891	Feb. 29, 1891	1 month.
Kennedy, J. P.	Canada	17	Boilermaker	Deer Lodge	Grand larceny	5 years	June 2, 1887	June 2, 1892	Mar. 2, 1891	1 yr 3 mos.
Driscoll, C.	New York	53	Miner	Deer Lodge	Forgery	1 year	April 12, 1890	April 12, 1891	Mar. 12, 1891	1 month.
Spitznagle, J.	Canada	23	Telegraph Operator	Deer Lodge	Grand larceny	1 year	April 12, 1890	April 12, 1891	Mar. 12, 1891	1 month.
Petty, R. W.	Illinois	31	Laborer	Deer Lodge	Assault to murder	1 year	April 15, 1890	April 15, 1891	Mar. 15, 1891	1 month.
McDougall, J.	Scotland	42	Boilermaker	Deer Lodge	Forgery	1 year	April 15, 1890	April 15, 1891	Mar. 15, 1891	1 month.
Grahame, M.	Kansas	24	Housekeeper	Fergus	Assault deadly wpn	1 year	April 15, 1890	April 15, 1891	Mar. 15, 1891	29 days.
Deardorf, S.	Pennsylvania	53	Wood Chopper	Deer Lodge	Obtaining money on false pretence	1 year	April 21, 1890	April 21, 1891	Mar. 21, 1891	1 month.
Ah-Gee	China	40	Cook	Deer Lodge	Forgery	1 year	April 21, 1890	April 21, 1891	Mar. 21, 1891	1 month.

TABLE C.—CONTINUED.

Name	Nativity	Age	Occupation	County Convicted In	Crime	Term of Sentence	Date of Sentence	Expiration of Sentence Without Good Time	Expiration of Sentence With Full Good Time	Good Time Allowed
Courtney, J	Illinois	19	Laborer	Silver Bow	Burglary	2 years	June 15, 1889	June 15, 1891	Mar. 15, 1891	2mos 20 ds
Dulin, W	Illinois	28	Telegraph Lineman	Silver Bow	Forgery	1 year	May 10, 1890	May 10, 1891	April 10, 1891	1 month
Sachs, D	Russia	30	Cook	Silver Bow	Embezzlement	1 year	May 20, 1890	May 20, 1891	April 20, 1891	1 month
Garr, J	Nebraska	20	Rancher	Beaverhead	Grand larceny	1 year	May 21, 1890	May 21, 1891	April 21, 1891	1 month
Murphy, Jas	Massachusetts	18	Laborer	Silver Bow	Burglary	2 years	May 18, 1889	May 18, 1891	Feb. 18, 1891	25 days
Namo, F	Canada	25	Laborer	Choteau	Grand larceny	1 year	May 24, 1890	May 24, 1891	April 24, 1891	1 month
Taske, P	Germany	4	Cook	Lewis and Clarke	Grand larceny	1 year	May 31, 1890	May 31, 1891	April 30, 1891	1 month
McCombe, J	Canada	20	Laborer	Silver Bow	Grand larceny	1 year	May 31, 1890	May 31, 1891	April 30, 1891	1 month
Sands, J	Michigan	23	Teamster	Silver Bow	Forgery	1 year	May 24, 1890	May 24, 1891	April 24, 1891	21 days
Cloudy, G	California	28	Blacksmith	Silver Bow	Forgery	5 years	Aug. 9, 1887	Aug. 9, 1892	May 9, 1891	15 months
Kennedy, A	New York	34	Farmer	Missoula	Grand larceny	18 months	Jan. 11, 1890	July 11, 1891	May 11, 1891	2 months
Partello, F	Mexico	30	Laborer	Yellowstone	Rape	5 years	Feb. 21, 1891	Feb. 21, 1896	Nov. 21, 1894	New trial May 13,'91
Cummins, T	New York	34	Laborer	Silver Bow	Grand larceny	1 year	June 14, 1890	June 14, 1891	May 14, 1891	1 month
Cary, N	Kentucky	20	Cook	Yellowstone	Robbery	5 years	April 25, 1889	April 25, 1894	Jan. 25, 1893	Pardoned May 14,'91
Green, D. T	New York	38	Jeweler	Gallatin	Grand larceny	3 years	June 18, 1889	June 18, 1892	Dec. 18, 1891	Pardoned May 14,'91
Blood	Montana	25	Indian	Choteau	Grand larceny	18 months	Jan. 17, 1890	July 17, 1891	May 17, 1891	2 months
Poney	Montana	10	Indian	Choteau	Grand larceny	18 months	Jan. 18, 1890	July 18, 1891	May 18, 1891	2 months
White Shell	Montana	26	Indian	Choteau	Grand larceny	18 months	Jan. 18, 1890	July 18, 1891	May 18, 1891	2 months
Con Strike	Montana	21	Indian	Choteau	Grand larceny	18 months	Jan. 18, 1890	July 18, 1891	May 18, 1891	2 months
Ryan, Jas	Pennsylvania	35	Laborer	Silver Bow	Forgery	3 years	Nov. 24, 1888	Nov. 24, 1891	May 44, 1891	6 months
Trout, J. P	Missouri	29	Laborer	Park	Assault deadly wpn	1 year	June 25, 1890	June 25, 1891	May 25, 1891	1 month
Harris, H. C	Michigan	24	Barber	Custer	Burglary	18 months	Feb. 3, 1890	Aug. 3, 1891	June 3, 1891	2 months
Starkie, B	West Indies	35	Clerk	Lewis and Clarke	Forgery	1 year	July 12, 1890	July 12, 1891	June 12, 1891	1 month
Tabor, B	N. Brunswick	19	Engineer	Missoula	Grand larceny	1 year	July 12, 1890	July 12, 1891	June 12, 1891	1 month
Ivory	Montana	20	Indian	Fergus	Grand larceny	8 years	April 4, 1887	April 4, 1895	July 4, 1892	Died
Barus, T	Massachusetts	21	Tinsmith	Park	Burglary	2 years	Sept. 27, 1889	Sept. 27, 1891	June 27, 1891	June 13,'91
Roberts, E	Missouri	22	Laborer	Park	Grand larceny	2 years	Sept. 27, 1889	Sept. 27, 1891	June 27, 1891	3 months
McGee, W	Missouri	27	Railroader	Beaverhead	Assault to murder	18 months	Feb. 20, 1890	Aug. 20, 1891	June 20, 1891	3 months
Ellis, R	Canada	27	Railroader	Park	Burglary	2 years	Sept. 27, 1889	Sept. 27, 1891	June 27, 1891	1 mo 20 ds
Zollman, C	Nebraska	22	Laborer	Beaverhead	Grand larceny	1 year	Aug. 14, 1890	Aug. 14, 1891	July 14, 1891	1 mo 21 ds
White, J. P	Vermont	27	Carpenter	Lewis and Clarke	Sodomy	5 years	Oct. 15, 1887	Oct. 15, 1892	July 15, 1891	15 months
Walker, W. B	Dakota	44	Cook	Beaverhead	Grand larceny	2 years	Oct. 9, 1889	Oct. 9, 1891	July 9, 1891	1 mo 19 ds
Lopus, T	California	27	Cigarmaker	Deer Lodge	Assault to do bodily injury	1 year	June 11, 1891	June 11, 1892	May 11, 1892	New trial July 22,'91

Name	Nativity	Age	Occupation	County	Crime	Term	Date of sentence	When received	Expiration of sentence	Remarks
Kingsley, A.	Missouri	26	Laborer	Deer Lodge	Grand larceny	5 years	April 11, 1891	April 11, 1891	Jan. 11, 1895	New trial July 27, '91
Walker, J.	Kansas	16	Waiter	Beaverhead	Burglary	1 year	Aug. 14, 1890	Aug. 14, 1891	July 14, '91	10 days
Hocker, M.	Ohio	33	Shoemaker	Gallatin	Resisting officer	1 year	Sept. 13, 1890	Sept. 13, 1891	Aug. 13, '91	1 month
Hod, F.	Pennsylvania	30	Railroader	Deer Lodge	Grand larceny	1 year	Sept. 20, 1890	Sept. 20, 1891	Aug. 20, 1891	1 month
Powers, T.	Massachusetts	32	File cutter	Silver Bow	Grand larceny	1 year	Sept. 22, 1890	Sept. 22, 1891	Aug. 22, 1891	1 month
Cordon, J.	Ohio	32	Moulder	Lewis and Clarke	Burglary	2 years	June 18, 1891	June 18, 1891	Mar. 18, 1893	Died Aug. 25, '91
Warn, A.	Sweden	23	Laborer	Cascade	Attempt to commit burglary	1 year	April 9, 1891	April 9, 1891	April 9, 1892	Mar. 9, 1892	In Asy.
Hancock, J.	Canada	32	Saloon Keeper	Dawson	Selling liquor to an Indian	1 year	Feb. 9, 1891	Feb. 9, 1891	Feb. 9, 1892	Jan. 9, 1892	Aug. 31, '91 Pardoned
Grimes, D.	California	29	Miner	Silver Bow	Assault to do bodily injury	1 year	Oct. 4, 1890	Oct. 4, 1891	Sept. 4, 1891	Sept. 2, '91 1 month
Reeves, W.	Ohio	23	Miner	Silver Bow	Grand larceny	1 year	Oct. 4, 1890	Oct. 4, 1891	Sept. 4, 1891	1 month
Wheeler, J.	Kentucky	34	Cabinet Maker	Silver Bow	Grand larceny	1 year	Oct. 4, 1890	Oct. 4, 1891	Sept. 4, 1891	1 month
Waugh, J. M.	Virginia	25	Wheelwright	Custer	Rape	5 years	Mar. 10, 1891	Mar. 10, 1894	Dec. 10, 1894	Sept. 3, '91 Pardoned
Hopkins, J.	New York	41	Actress	Jefferson	Assault deadly wpn	1 year	Oct. 6, 1890	Oct. 6, 1891	Sept. 6, 1891	Sept. 3, '91 1 month
McArthur, D.	Canada	39	Painter	Missoula	Assault deadly wpn	2 years	Dec. 7, 1889	Dec. 7, 1891	Sept. 7, 1891	3 months
O'Donnell, E.	Missouri	20	Miner	Deer Lodge	Obtaining valuable papers false pretence	18 months	Nov. 10, 1890	Nov. 10, 1891	May 10, 1891	2 months
Smith, J. B.	Texas	25	Cook	Silver Bow	Assault to do bodily injury	2 months	Nov. 10, 1890	Nov. 10, 1891	Sept. 10, 1891	2 months
Freeman, C.	New York	37	Blacksmith	Silver Bow	Grand larceny	1 year	Oct. 1, 1890	Oct. 1, 1891	Sept. 4, 1891	13 days
Murphy, T.	Ireland	10	Laborer	Cascade	Grand larceny	1 year	Oct. 13, 1890	Oct. 13, 1891	Sept. 13, 1891	1 month
Scanlan, W.	Wisconsin	22	Painter	Lewis and Clarke	Grand larceny	18 months	May 14, 1890	Nov. 14, 1891	Sept. 14, 1891	2 months
Howard, J. E.	Iowa	34	Rancher	Missoula	Grand larceny	1 year	Oct. 18, 1890	Oct. 18, 1891	Sept. 18, 1891	1 month
Garing, W.	Pennsylvania	30	Cigarmaker	Silver Bow	Forgery	2 years	Oct. 20, 1890	Sept. 22, 1892	June 22, 1892	Habeas corpus
Rogers, C.	Texas	26	Cowboy	Cascade	Forgery	3 years	May 29, 1889	May 29, 1892	Nov. 29, 1891	Sept. 20, '91 Died Sept. 21, '91
King, J. W.	Kentucky	32	Carpenter	Park	Forgery	1 year	Oct. 25, 1890	Oct. 25, 1891	Sept. 25, 1891	1 month
McLeary, L.	Ireland	30	Railroader	Park	Burglary	1 year	Oct. 25, 1890	Oct. 25, 1891	Sept. 25, 1891	1 month
Morgan, J. F.	New Jersey	21	Laborer	Gallatin	Attempt to break jail	2 years	Dec. 26, 1890	Dec. 26, 1891	Sept. 26, 1891	3 months
Boyle, J.	Pennsylvania	12	Laborer	Cascade	Grand larceny	1 year	Oct. 28, 1890	Oct. 28, 1891	Sept. 28, 1891	1 month
Sicott, L.	Iowa	26	Railroader	Cascade	Embezzlement	1 year	Oct. 28, 1890	Oct. 28, 1891	Sept. 28, 1891	1 month
Harmon, W.	Missouri	30	Teamster	Choteau	Grand larceny	1 year	Nov. 13, 1890	Nov. 13, 1891	Oct. 13, 1891	1 month
Hatry Coat.	Montana	22	Indian	Choteau	Grand larceny	1 year	Nov. 13, 1890	Nov. 13, 1891	Oct. 13, 1891	1 month
Trevrier, N.	Canada	27	Laborer	Choteau	Grand larceny	1 year	Nov. 13, 1890	Nov. 13, 1891	Oct. 13, 1891	1 month
Paul, Harry	Washington	23	Indian	Missoula	Grand larceny	1 year	Oct. 17, 1890	Oct. 17, 1891	Sept. 17, 1891	1 month
Russell, E.	Iowa	30	Laborer	Missoula	Burglary	1 year	Nov. 17, 1890	Nov. 17, 1891	Oct. 17, 1891	None
Kabolin, N.	Austria	45	Laborer	Deer Lodge	Assault deadly wpn	2 years	Jan. 18, 1891	Jan. 18, 1891	Oct. 18, 1891	3 months
Ah Yuen,	China	42	Miner	Beaverhead	Assault deadly wpn	1 year	Nov. 10, 1890	Nov. 10, 1891	Oct. 10, 1891	3 months
Johnson, F.	California	32	Laborer	Missoula	Grand larceny	1 year	Nov. 22, 1890	Nov. 22, 1891	Oct. 22, 1891	1 month
Stapp, C.	Ohio	32	Butcher	Missoula	Grand larceny	1 year	Nov. 22, 1890	Nov. 22, 1891	Oct. 22, 1891	1 month

TABLE C.—CONCLUDED.

Name	Nativity	Age	Occupation	County Convicted In.	Crime	Term of Sentence.	Date of Sentence.	Expiration of Sentence Without Good Time.	Expiration of Sentence With Full Good Time.	Good Time Allowed.
Hoppe, M.	Germany	24	Watchmaker	Choteau	Murder	20 years	Nov. 26, 1888	Nov. 26, 1908	Feb. 26, 1899	In. Asy. Oct. 24, '91.
Gillespie, M.	Ohio	29	Laborer	Missoula	Assault deadly wpn	1 year	Dec. 1, 1890	Dec. 1, 1891	Nov. 1, 1891	1 month.
Heaston, C. A.	Utah	24	Clerk	Silver Bow	Attempt to utter forged check	3 years	May 10, 1889	May 10, 1892	Nov. 10, 1891	6 months.
Rutledge, Jos.	Missouri	26	Laborer	Missoula	Grand larceny	1 year	Nov. 22, 1890	Nov. 22, 1891	Oct. 22, 1891	None.
Fitzgerald, J.	New York	24	Laborer	Meagher	Burglary	4 years	Sept. 19, 1888	Sept. 19, 1892	Nov. 19, 1891	9 ms 20 ds.

TABLE D.

Showing Amount of Money Belonging to Prisoners Confined in Montana State Penitentiary, at Deer Lodge, Montana, in hands of Conley and McTague, Prison Contractors, December 1, 1891.

Name.	Amount.	Name.	Amount.
Ah Wing, (No. 1)	$5 30	Jordan, Eugene	$12 10
Ah Wing, (No. 2)	2 15	Johnson, Peter A	1 15
Anderson, Robt. F	12	Jessup, Alexander	181 31
Ah Tek	40	Jackson, John	40
Bond, John M	5	Jaggers, Joseph	36 65
Bennett, Rose	27 45	Jones, William W	5 80
Boyer, Alfred	1 30	Jones, Chas. M	30
Brazier, Albert E	3 55	Jim Wah Chung	5 90
Brown, Martin	6 85	Kasson, Walter F	44 80
Blair, Jacob	35	Kelley, John A	2 40
Bray, John	30	Keefe, John	75
Brady, Frank	3 05	Kooken, Pierce	1 50
Bryant, Chas. W	5 40	Kelley, Joseph	2 25
Bright, George	10 05	Lonink, Nathan L	5
Burns, Thomas	6 70	Leeper, Hugh	5
Briyd, Frank	75	Lumpp, Henry	21 50
Breen, Jean	4 20	Linnebarger, Wm. H	3 40
Baker, James	11 95	Lohmer, Charles	5 00
Burns, William	4 00	Lynch, Tim	20
Clayton, Charles	160 90	Langdon, Frank	50
Conneily, Michael	75	Lovegreen, Augustus	7 60
Campbell, Joseph	8 45	Leitch, Thomas	33 60
Campbell, James	11 65	Lee, John	4 75
Cutler, Arthur	21 65	Lewis, Edwin J	6 65
Conley, John	5	Miller, John	37 75
Click, Henry	20	Manton, Dennis	35 04
Canning, John	25	Morgan, Fred. J	3 05
Callahan, John	3 10	Maguire, Charles	6 20
Carton, Matthew	10 65	McKenzie, Edwin H	5
Clark, Henry	5 00	McDonald, William R	5 55
Doyle, Douglass	1 45	McLaughlin, John	20 60
Duffy, Charles	10	McNamara, Pat'k J	12 60
Dolan, James	2 60	McGill, Charles B	1 20
Dearborn, William A	7 70	McMahon, Patrick	4 35
Devine, Charles	1 55	Miller, William	4 25
Durbon, William	14 50	McGovern, James	30 15
Edmonson, Henry	7 05	McCormick, Thomas	5
Easton, William	1 31	Mosier, Urban	25
Estes, Mary	1 10	McLin, James B	40
Fitzgerald, Michael	48 40	Manning, Harry	40
Fuller, Harry	1 00	McCarthy, John	1 85
Flynn, William	16 45	McDonald, Lewis H	2
Frederickson, Wm. H	16 70	Morgan, James	1 50
Field, James	05	Monroe, Sidney	50
Fisher, Clarence	10	McLaughlin, Terrence	1 00
Fenton, Wm. H	5 05	Nelson, James	12 00
Fitzpatrick, Patrick	45	Nash, William	15
Fish, James	11 00	Neiman, Edward	1 00
Gilbert, George	1 80	O'Brien, James	10
Gendron, Antoine	10	Olson, Charles	2 55
Gibbs, James W	8 00	Overman, Charles	6 60
Gore, Fred. J. T	4 55	Ormond, Thomas	50
Griffin, John	25	O'Neill, Frank	15 00
Grant, Archie	20 55	Pendry, Reuben	4 30
Gray, Frank	50	Phillip, John	9 10
Gaffney, Frank	56 25	Page, Wm. H	18 65
Hurst, Henry	3 50	Phelps, John	2 70
Hallenbeck, Edward L	27 68	Quinn, Michael	4 50
Havens, Merritt S	3 15	Russell, Stewart	8 10
Hawkes, Daniel	1 05	Reub, Albert	2 35
Herriman, Henry R	55	Rhodes, Willis	9 18
Hannaway, Charles B	2 55	Riley, William J	25 12
Haggerty, John	5	Rowand, John A	3 87
Hennessey, John F	6 65	Root, William H	15
Hofke, Albert	25	Raney, Curley	10 00

TABLE D—Concluded.

Name.	Amount.	Name.	Amount.
Russell, Robert...	$0 10	Smith, Charles A....................	$1 80
Sterling, John.......................	1 65	Titus, Daniel	4 40
Sasson, Herman.....................	7 40	Trushel, Frank	40 15
Shank, Lewis.......................	1 77	Thomas, Howell.....................	5 05
Straight, Harry W	3 00	Teets, James A	65
Sullivan, John	7 05	Thompson, William.................	40
Smith, Charles A	1 55	Thomas, William	8 10
Salmon, John	10 55	Teichart, Carl	21 50
Shedd, Lester.......................	4 80	Troudelle, Peter	6 70
Smith, James (No. 1)	5	Thurston, Henry	5
Schroeder, Frederick	5	You Loy..........	4 05
Street, John S................	5	Warren, Alva J.....................	25
Scheel, John R	20	Warren, Alva J.....................	14 35
Schneider, John.....................	11 00	Whaley, Thomas	1 50
Slaussen, Andrew	25	Williams, John (No. 1).............	1 85
Strider, George.....................	4 15	Williams, Frank....................	8 75
Smith, Osceola	18 60		
Shatto, George	50	Total	$1,503 21

TABLE E.

Statement of Prisoners Treated by the Prison Physician in Montana State Penitentiary, at Deer Lodge, Montana, from November 1, 1891, to December 1, 1891.

NAME OF CONVICT.	Disease, Nature of.	Treatment, Nature of.	Result.	When Sent to Hospital.	When Discharged.	In Case of Death, Age.	Remarks.
Brown, Edward	Gastro Duodenal Catarrh	Antiseptic Hygiene		No Hospital Here.			
Brady, Florence	Second Syphilis	Mixed					
Bennett, Rose	Second Syphilis	Mixed					
Bennington, Richard	Spermatorrhœa	Sedative Tonic					
Evans, Frank L.	Mital Regurgitation without Artic in Sufficiency	Tonic, Sedative, Hygiene					
Fitzgerald, Michael	Second Syphilis	Mixed					
Finlay, Larra	Rheumatism	Counter Irritant, Constitutional	Cured				
Gray, Frank	Stricture	Surgical					
Hill, Fred W	Tonsolitis	Astringents	Cured				
Havens, Merritt S.	Second Syphilis	Mixed					
Leitch, Thomas E.	Agina Pectoris	Tonic, Sedative	Cured				
Lamb, John E.	Rheumatism	Counter Irritant, Constitutional	Cured				
Linnecharger, Frank	Nephritis	Counter Irritant, Constitutional	Cured				
Nelson, James	Rheumatism	Counter Irritant, Constitutional	Cured				
Murray, Andrew	Post Nasal Catarrh	Douche	Cured				
Oleson, Charles	Indigestion	Digestive Agents	Cured				
Powers, Robert	Feigned Insanity	Dungeon	Cured				
Russell, Edward	Gleet	Local Constitutional					
Sullivan, John	Cystitis	Diuretic Sedative	Cured				
Williams, Frank	Tonsolitis	Astringents	Cured				

TABLE F.

Showing Expenses Incurred by the State Board of Prison Commissioners, between the Fifth day of June, 1891, and the First day of December, 1891.

From Whom Purchased.	When Purchased.	For What Object Expense Was Incurred.	Value.	When Paid.	Remarks.
Pioneer Press Company	June 5	Expenses of Attorney General Visiting Prison.	$1 00	June 16	Paid from Attorney General's Expense Acc't
Pioneer Press Company	July 30	1 Hospital Register	14 50	Aug. 19	Paid from House Bill 76
Pioneer Press Company	July 30	1 Convict Register	34 00	Aug. 19	Paid from House Bill 76
Pioneer Press Company	July 30	1 Valuable and Money Register	14 50	Aug. 19	Paid from House Bill 76
Pioneer Press Company	July 30	1 Department Register	11 00	Aug. 19	Paid from House Bill 76
		Express on same	9 10	Aug. 19	Paid from House Bill 76
Independent Publishing Co.	Sept. 21	1,000 Copies State Prison Rules	205 00	Sept. 21	Paid from House Bill 76
Journal Publishing Co.	Sept. 21	1 Valuable and Money Register	13 00	Sept. 21	Paid from House Bill 76
Journal Publishing Co.	Oct. 26	1,000 Statements of Clothing	10 50	Oct. 20	Paid from House Bill 76
Journal Publishing Co.	Oct. 17	1 Visitors Register	13 00	Oct. 20	Paid from House Bill 76
Journal Publishing Co.	Oct. 20	1 Cash Book	0 00	Oct. 20	Paid from House Bill 76
Journal Publishing Co.	Oct. 12	1 Journal	10 50	Oct. 20	Paid from House Bill 76
Journal Publishing Co.	Nov. 9	1,000 Circular Letter	4 00	Nov. 17	Expense Account
Journal Publishing Co.	Nov. 14	500 Envelopes	11 50	Nov. 17	Expense Account
Journal Publishing Co.	Nov. 14	Description Book	23 00	Nov. 17	Expense Account
Journal Publishing Co.	Nov. 14	Ledger	23 00	Nov. 17	Expense Account

SECOND ANNUAL REPORT

OF THE

BOARD OF STATE

Prison Commissioners,

OF THE

State of Montana,

December 1, 1892.

INDEPENDENT PUB. CO.,
HELENA, MONTANA.
1892.

SECOND ANNUAL REPORT.

OFFICE STATE BOARD OF PRISON COMMISSIONERS,
HELENA, Montana, Dec. 1, 1892.

To His Excellency, Joseph K. Toole, Governor of Montana:

In compliance with the laws of the State of Montana, the State Board of Prison Commissioners respectfully submit this their second annual report of the management and condition of the State Prison situated at Deer Lodge, State of Montana, for the fiscal year ending December 1, 1892.

During the year the affairs of the prison have been conducted in a very satisfactory manner. The establishment has been kept clean and in good order and many improvements and additions made thereto.

The prison has been in operation since the year 1871. At that time the north wing of what is now the Montana State Prison was built by the Federal government and was donated to the Territory of Montana. It then consisted of a stone building 68x40 feet, with a double tier of brick cells numbering in all twenty-eight, with a capacity of fifty-six. Shortly afterwards it passed under the control of the United States government which entered into a contract with the Territory of Montana to maintain all territorial prisoners, first at $1, then at 85 cents, then at 75 cents per capita per diem, which contract at the latter price was maintained up to March, 1890. The middle building which is of stone, 35x50 feet, three stories, as well as the south wing was built by the United States government, and was completed in 1886. The middle building is used as sleeping quarters for guards, guards' kitchen and dining room, warden's office and visitors' reception room. The south wing which is 68x40 feet, three stories, contains a three-tier block of brick cells, numbering in all forty-two, with a capacity of eighty-four. In 1889 the United States government also erected a brick building 18x24 feet as quarters for female prisoners; its capacity is eight.

On the admission of the Territory of Montana to the Union, the above described property together with twenty acres of ground in connection therewith, and all outbuildings erected thereon, became the property of the State of Montana by gift from the United States. In February, 1890, a contract for the keeping and maintaining of all State prisoners was entered into between the State and Messrs. Conley and McTague at the rate of 70 cents per capita per diem for the first one hundred, and 65 cents per capita per diem for all over that number, which contract was for a term of one year. On March 9, 1891, the Governor for and on behalf of the State, entered into a contract with Messrs. Conley and McTague to care for the prisoners in the State Prison until March 1, 1893, (at the same rate specified in the former contract) which contract is still in force and effect.

Since acquiring the above property the State Board of Prison Commissioners of Montana, have caused to be erected a third tier of wooden cells, with grated doors and lined with sheet iron, in the north wing of the prison, which cells have a capacity of 42.

Other additions in the way of improvements have been made from time to time as the necessity for them became apparent. In the year 1882, and again in 1885 the kitchen of the prison, which was merely a frame structure, burned down. The fire originated by grease constantly flying from the stove against the rafters and logs to such an extent that the wood and timbers had become partially soaked with grease, which the sparks from the stove ignited, thus consuming the building on the dates above mentioned. The maintaining of a wooden building for a kitchen which was erected alongside of and against the north wing of the prison, was a standing menace against the safety and security of the other buildings, and as well the prisoners therein confined.

A brick building was therefore erected, 20x24 feet, having a stone foundation. Inside the kitchen was built an oven 10x14, which has baking capacity sufficient to feed 600 persons.

The old dining room of the prison was located south of the south wing of the prison, dimensions 20x30 feet, having been built in the spring of 1890. Owing to the increase of prisoners it was deemed necessary to construct a larger dining room, and accordingly in September, 1891, the old one was moved to a building which is 150 feet southwest of the south wing of the prison. This building was enlarged by an addition of thirty feet in length, making the present building 20x60 feet, with a seating capacity of 230 persons.

In October, 1890, it became necessary to erect a small log building for the purpose of furnishing facilities for the prison physician to examine prisoners separate and apart from the others, also to provide a place for medicines. The building which was erected is 16x30 feet and contains an operating table.

On March 19, 1892, the overcrowded condition of the prison rendered it necessary to put in a boiler and heater for bathing purposes. Sufficient water can be heated to bathe 600 men each day, and is so arranged that five men can bath at one time.

From time to time additions and improvements have been made, including:

In 1890 a milk house, built at the recommendation of the prison physician, to furnish the prisoners with oatmeal and milk three times each week. In compliance with this recommendation, eighteen cows were purchased by the prison contractors;

A root cellar, for the purpose of holding vegetables sufficient to feed the prisoners for a year;

Three lookouts, for the accommodation of the day and night guards, erected in different corners of the prison yard;

Repairing fences and roof and building new south fence;

Putting in water plant, or water works, in the prison yard, and also putting in water basins for the use of the prisoners in the new cell building, and bringing the pipes into the several wings of the prison, kitchen, wash-house and surgery;

In 1891, a store house, in which to keep provisions and clothing for the prisoners, in compliance with Rule 64, requiring the contractors to preserve all clothing belonging to prisoners whose term did not exceed three years;

A new cell house, with a capacity of 164, for the accommodation of prisonors who, owing to the already crowded condition of the prison proper, could not be confined therein;

Painting buildings, in the process of which two barrels of paint were consumed;

In 1892, laying new flooring in the main hall, galleries and guards' kitchen;

Constructing new dark cells and putting an electric light in the prison yard to furnish light throughout the premises, besides several minor improvements unnecessary to enumerate.

———

Industry is one of the first lessons that should be taught in a prison. Work is one of the greatest reformers and the chief aid to the reformation of a man is to teach him to make his living. The thing to be attained, if possible, is such an employment or trade as may be useful to a man when he is discharged, and at the same time, proper opportunity should be given for such mental culture as may help to eradicate crime. It must be borne in mind that a large proportion of the convicts are uneducated, illiterate men, some never having attended school or had an opportunity to exercise their mind or brain powers but to a small extent.

Should they be kept shut up and allowed to remain in a perfectly dormant condition, they would be likely to lose control of their mental powers.

Of necessity, owing to the cramped condition of the prison at the present time, and the large number of prisoners therein confined, no very decisive steps can be taken in this matter; but, in this connection we would strenuously urge the establishment of schools in the prison, where not only the common school branches might be taught, but where those prisoners of a higher, more intellectual class might have an opportunity of learning shorthand, typewriting or telegraphy, and we would ask that a typewriter and at least two telegraph instruments be supplied for their use, which would necessitate an appropriation of $200.

It does not seem right that men should be kept in the prison during the best part of their lives and then set adrift in the world without means or knowledge whereby they might obtain a livelihood; it is not fair to these men, nor is it just that nothing should be taught them while in prison, that nothing should be done to occupy their minds or time.

What wonder is it that prisoners being released from confinement fall into their old associations and are convicted a second time. On the other hand, if they were taught while in prison, to make a living, or their mental condition was elevated, they would not, upon their discharge, be so likely to be exposed to temptation arising from want.

We would strongly advocate the setting aside of an appropriation of $150 to be used in the purchase of books for the prisoners. In addition to school books or text books, books of history, travel and biography would be beneficial, and at the same time highly enjoyable to the prisoners, some of whom are quite well read and informed and sorely miss the advantage of access to a library.

With a view to obtain reading matter for the use of the prisoners now confined in the State Prison, we transmitted, under date of November 19, 1892, circular letters to the publisher of each weekly newspaper in Montana, requesting that a copy of each weekly edition be sent to the penitentiary, through the Board of Prison Commissioners. As no appropriation had been set aside for this purpose we requested that, if consistent, the publishers should consider the copies so furnished as a donation for the use and benefit of the prisoners. In nearly every instance replies to this communication were favorable, but nevertheless, it seems only fair and we would earnestly request that an appropriation of $150 be set apart for the purpose of paying the subscription price of these newspapers so mentioned.

As the solution of all of these questions herein set out properly belongs to the Legislative Assembly, we would earnestly recommend that this body, petitioned by the State Board of Prison Commissioners, shall see fit to appropriate a sum of money sufficient to carry out and put into execution the suggestions and matters above referred to.

The facts of the fiscal year ending December 1, 1892, concerning the prisoners and the affairs of the prison are given in twenty-five tables, which follow and to which attention is especially invited.

Table No. 1 gives the birthplace of prisoners confined in the State Prison.

Table No. 2 shows the commitments as classed by counties. The greatest number, eighty, having been convicted in Silver Bow county, and the smallest number, one, in Dawson county.

Table No. 3 shows the term of sentence of prisoners confined in the State Prison. One year is the shortest sentence imposed upon any of the prisoners therein, and nineteen prisoners are sentenced for life.

Table No. 4 shows the occupations of the prisoners. It will be seen that the majority lay claim to being skilled mechanics or to having a "trade," but the greater number of these are not masters of the trades they claim as theirs, but have only a rudimentary knowledge of them.

Table No. 5 shows the offenses for which persons have been committed to the penitentiary. It will be observed that offences against the property are more in proportion than the other two.

Table No. 6 shows the marriage condition of the prisoners; from which it will be seen that a large majority are single men.

Table No. 7 shows under what process the prisoners were convicted.

Table No. 8 shows the ages of the prisoners. Attention is called to the proportion of commitments of persons under twenty years of age. This fact emphasizes the necessity of teaching and training here.

Table No. 9 shows the number of prisoners treated by the prison physician and the disease for which they were treated.

Table No. 10, being a continuation of Table No. 9, shows the number of days, weeks or months each prisoner was treated by the physician.

Table No. 11 shows the number of prisoners punished for violation of rules and the number of the rule violated.

Table No. 12 shows the mode and extent of punishment of the prisoners who have violated the rules of the prison.

Table No. 13 shows the number of prisoners confined in the State Prison who cannot read, cannot write, those who have attended school not to exceed one year, those who have attended school not to exceed six months and those who have never attended school at all.

Table No. 14 shows the term of sentence of the prisoners described in the above table, viz: those who cannot read, cannot write, etc.

Table No. 15 shows the financial condition of the prisoners confined in the State Prison.

Table No. 16 shows the process of release of prisoners for the fiscal year ending December 1, 1892, whether discharged by expiration of sentence, pardon, etc.

Table No. 17 shows the length of "good time" allowed prisoners; the Statute and the Rules of the Prison having provided that every prisoner who shall conduct himself in an orderly and peaceable manner, shall be entitled to diminution of time from his sentence.

Tables No. 18 and 19 show the amount of expenditures in furnishing discharged prisoners with cash gratuity and suitable clothing and the number of prisoners so supplied.

Table No. 20 shows the number of previous commitments of prisoners received during the year and in previous years.

Table No. 21 shows the conduct of prisoners while in prison, who have since been discharged.

Table No. 22 shows the number of prisoners who were convicted prior to December 1, 1891: number received since that date; number released during the fiscal year ending December 1, 1892, and the number remaining in custody on the 1st day of December, 1892.

Table No. 23 shows the number of prisoners confined in the State Prison for each year since the organization of the State Prison in 1892.

Table "A" shows the amount paid contractors monthly for the keeping of convicts for the fiscal year commencing December 1, 1891, and ending December 1, 1892, and the amount paid out monthly for clothing for discharged convicts and the amount of money paid out to such convicts during said fiscal year.

Table "B" shows the name of the Sheriff of each county, county wherein prisoner was sentenced, date of admission at prison, mileage allowed Sheriff for transporting each convict and the amount so allowed, mileage allowed Sheriff to and from prison and the amount so allowed, total number of prisoners taken from each county, and total amount allowed each Sheriff for the fiscal year ending December 1, 1892.

Table "C" refers merely to the State Board of Prison Commissioners and is an account of the expenses incurred by them during the fiscal year ending December 1, 1892.

A reference to the records of the State Prison reveals the following facts, and we draw the following conclusions therefrom:

The monthly expenses for the care and maintenance of prisoners for the month ending November 30, 1889, were $3,965.25, while those for the month ending November 30, 1892, were $8,162.20. The report for the month ending November 30, 1889, shows that the number of prisoners in the State Prison

at that time was 178: while the report for the month ending
November 30, 1892, shows that there were 343 prisoners in the
penitentiary.

We find that the increase of prisoners for the year 1892 is al-
most double the number of prisoners convicted during the year
1889, while the expense for caring and maintaining them for the
month ending November 1, 1892, is more than double that for
the month ending November 1, 1889.

Reckoning on this basis it is fair to presume that the number
of prisoners for the next fiscal year, ending December 1, 1893,
will exceed 375, while the expense of keeping the same will
probably amount to the sum of $100,000: and the expense for
the fiscal year, ending December 1, 1894, $125,000.

We would present this as a suggestion to your Excellency, and
the Legislative Assembly, in order that they may have before
them some estimate of what the probable cost of maintaining
prisoners in the penitentiary for the next two years will be, and
thus make sufficient appropriation for the same.

To the end that the business and work connected with this
department may be transacted with method and dispatch, all
means and facilities so to do should be readily furnished the board
by the law-making power. We would therefore recommend in
this connection, that the board be legally authorized to employ a
clerk, at a salary of $1,200 per annum for the performance of
the duties arising thereunder.

It may be here noted that Rule 73 of "Rules and Regulations
for the Government of the Montana State Prison," requires that
the contractor shall, not more that ten nor less than seven days
prior to the expiration of the term of imprisonment of any prisoner in the said prison, furnish the President of the board with a
statement showing:

1. Name of prisoner to be discharged.
2. The term of sentence.
3. Good time granted by the board.
4. The date of discharge.
5. The kind of clothing, and condition thereof, belonging to
the prisoner.
6. The amount of valuables belonging to the prisoner when
committed.
7. The amount earned while in prison.

8. The amount of money expended for the prisoner's use.

9. The amount of money or valuables to the credit of the prisoner.

This statement must be filled out on a blank form prepared by the board.

The findings in each case having been made, they are required to be entered upon the records of the board, which necessitates much clerical assistance. We trust that the Legislature will, after a careful inquiry into and examination of the duties of the department, be satisfied that the necessity for the employment of clerical assistance for this board exists, and that they will see fit to set apart an appropriation sufficient to pay for the services so required.

Respectfully submitted,

JOSEPH K. TOOLE,

. Governor and President of the Board.

H. J. HASKELL,

Attorney General.

L. ROTWITT,

Secretary of State and Secretary of the Board.

Members of the State Board of Prison Commissioners.

MAY CUTHBERT,

Clerk of the Board.

STATISTICAL TABLES

RELATING TO THE PRISONERS

IN THE STATE PRISON.

TABLE NO. 1.

Showing Nativities of Prisoners Confined in the State Prison up to December 1, 1892.

UNITED STATES.			
Alabama	2	Oregon	2
California	13	Pennsylvania	16
Colorado	2	Tennessee	1
Connecticut	1	Texas	6
Florida	2	Utah	4
Idaho	1	Vermont	2
Illinois	17	Virginia	7
Indiana	2	Washington, D. C	1
Indian Country	5	Wisconsin	9
Indian Territory	1	**FOREIGN LANDS.**	
Iowa	7		
Kansas	1	Canada	21
Kentucky	6	China	5
Louisiana	2	East Indies	1
Maine	3	England	11
Maryland	5	Finland	4
Massachusetts	17	France	2
Michigan	17	Germany	12
Minnesota	12	Holland	1
Mississipi	1	Ireland	23
Missouri	16	Italy	1
Montana	7	North Wales	1
Nevada	1	Norway	2
New Jersey	3	Ocean	1
New York	17	Scotland	4
North Carolina	1	Sweden	3
Ohio	11	Total	343

TABLE NO. 2.

Showing in what County the Prisoners Confined in the State Prison up to December 1, 1892, Were Convicted.

Beaverhead	18	Lewis and Clarke	51
Cascade	20	Madison	2
Choteau	31	Meagher	7
Custer	13	Missoula	26
Dawson	1	Park	26
Deer Lodge	20	Silver Bow	80
Fergus	13	Yellowstone	15
Gallatin	1		
Jefferson	8	Total	343

TABLE NO. 3.

Showing the Term of Sentence of each Prisoner Confined in State Prison up to December 1, 1892.

One year	60	Seven years	8
One year and two months	1	Seven years and six months	4
One year and five months	1	Eight years	8
One year and six months	21	Nine years	1
One year and nine months	2	Ten years	24
Two years	18	Eleven years	1
Two years and three months	1	Twelve years	5
Two years and six months	4	Fourteen years	1
Two years and nine months	1	Fifteen years	5
Three years	30	Eighteen years	4
Three years and six months	3	Twenty years	2
Four years	18	Twenty-two years	1
Four years and six months	2	Twenty-five years	2
Five years	39	Thirty years	1
Five years and three months	1	Forty years	1
Five years and six months	2	Life	10
Six years	11		
Six years and six months	2	Total	343

TABLE NO. 4.

Showing the Occupation of the Prisoners Now Confined in the State Prison.

Bakers	1	Lumbermen	2
Barbers	11	Machinists	5
Bartenders	1	Miller	1
Blacksmiths	5	Miners	27
Boilermaker	1	Moulders	2
Bookkeepers	2	Painters	3
Bricklayers	1	Physicians	2
Brickmaker	1	Plasterers	2
Butchers	1	Plumbers	6
Cabinet makers	3	Potter	1
Canvasser	1	Printers	5
Carpenters	6	Railroad carpenter	1
Cigarmakers	3	Railroaders	9
Clerks	5	Rivet maker	1
Cooks	22	Sailor	1
Cooper	1	Salesmen	2
Cowboys	18	Sheep herder	1
Dairyman	1	Shirt maker	1
Druggist	1	Shoemakers	8
Engineers	4	Stage artist	1
Farmers	21	Steamfitters	2
Firemen	3	Steel worker	1
Glass blowers	2	Stenographer	1
Harness maker	1	Stockraiser	1
Herb doctor	1	Stonecutter	1
Herders	4	Stonemasons	2
Horsemen	3	Tailors	3
Interior decorator	1	Teamsters	4
Iron moulders	2	Telegraph operators	2
Iron roller	1	Variety actor	1
Iron workers	2	Waiters	11
Jewelers	2	Without occupation	16
Laborers	70		
Laundrymen	3	Total	343
Lineman	1		

TABLE NO. 5.

Showing Crimes Committed by Prisoners Confined in the State Prison up to December 1, 1892.

Against the Person—		**Against Property—**	
Administering poison	1	Embezzlement	2
Assault to injure	2	Forgery	32
Assault on jailor	1	Grand larceny	63
Assault to kill	10	Obstructing railroad	2
Assault to rape	3	Obtaining money under false pretenses	2
Assault to rob	3	Receiving stolen property	2
Assault with deadly weapon	4		
Manslaughter	10	**Against Public Order and Decency—**	
Murder, first degree	4	Attempt to break jail	3
Murder, second degree	36	Conducting unlawful game	2
Rape	2	Escaping prison	7
Robbery	12	Fraudulent voting	1
		Infamous crime	2
Against Property—		Perjury	2
Assault to commit arson	1	Using explosives to catch fish	1
Arson	1		
Arson, third degree	2	Total	343
Attempt to commit burglary	2		
Burglary	100		

TABLE NO. 6.

Showing whether the Prisoners Confined in the State Prison up to December 1, 1892, are Married or Single.

Married...	50
Single..	279
Widowers..	13
Unknown...	1
Total...	343

TABLE NO. 7.

Showing Under What Process Conviction of the Prisoners Now Confined in State Prison Was Had.

Indictment..	209
Information.	85
Not given...	49
Total...	343

TABLE NO. 8.

Showing the Age of Prisoners Confined in the State Prison up to December 1, 1892.

From 15 to 20 years.....................	34	From 50 to 60 years................	6
20 to 25 years.......................	93	60 to 70 years....................	2
25 to 30 years.......................	83	Unknown	2
30 to 40 years.......................	91		
40 to 50 years	27	Total	343

TABLE NO. 9.

Showing the Number of Prisoners Treated by the Prison Physician from December 1, 1891, to December 1, 1892, and the Nature of the Disease.

Disease	No.	Disease	No.
Asthma	2	Pleurisy	1
Bronchitis	44	Pectoris	1
Cataract of Eye	1	Pharyngitis	1
Catarrh	18	Quincy	1
Catarrhal Pneumonia	1	Rheumatism	39
Chancroids	1	Rheumatism, Inflamatory	2
Cystitis	13	Rheumatism, Sciatic	1
Erysipelas	1	Scrofula	1
Feigned Insanity	1	Syphilis, Secondary	11
Gleet	1	Syphilitic Liploma Genitalis	1
Grippe	16	Tonsolitis	43
Gonorrhœa	3	Tuberculosis	2
Indigestior	15		
Neuralgia	1	Total	222

TABLE NO. 10.

Showing the Number of Days Each Prisoner Was Treated by the Prison Physician from December 1, 1891, to December 1, 1892.

2 Prisoners treated	2 days each	1 Prisoner treated	20 days each
6 Prisoners treated	3 "	1 Prisoner treated	21 "
14 Prisoners treated	4 "	1 Prisoner treated	22 "
14 Prisoners treated	5 "	3 Prisoners treated	23 "
20 Prisoners treated	6 "	3 Prisoners treated	27 "
36 Prisoners treated	7 "	1 Prisoner treated	28 "
27 Prisoners treated	8 "	1 Prisoner treated	33 "
15 Prisoners treated	9 "	1 Prisoner treated	36 "
12 Prisoners treated	10 "	2 Prisoners treated	40 "
4 Prisoners treated	11 "	1 Prisoner treated	46 "
6 Prisoners treated	12 "	1 Prisoner treated	49 "
6 Prisoners treated	13 "	1 Prisoner treated	53 "
9 Prisoners treated	14 "	1 Prisoner treated	58 "
6 Prisoners treated	15 "	1 Prisoner treated	61 "
1 Prisoner treated	16 "	1 Prisoner treated	66 "
1 Prisoner treated	17 "	1 Prisoner treated	11 months.
4 Prisoners treated	18 "	1 Prisoner treated	9 mos 11 ds.
1 Prisoner treated	19 "	16 Prisoners treated	

Total number of prisoners treated by prison physician, 222.

TABLE NO. 11.

Showing the Number of Prisoners Punished for Violation of Rules and the Number of the Rule Violated.

Rule 46 violated by	20 prisoners	Rule 82 violated by.............	1	prisoners
49 violated by	2 "	91 vialated by.............	2	"
50 violated by.............	1 "	103 violated by.............	6	"
52 violated by.............	28 "	104 violated by.............	7	"
54 violated by.............	23 "	107 violated by	38	"
57 violated by.............	11 "			
64 violated by.............	1 "	Total number violating rules ...	140	

TABLE NO. 12.

Showing the Mode and Extent of Punishment of the Prisoners Confined in the State Prison During the Fiscal year Ending December 1, 1892.

1 Dark cell, bread and water........	2 days	1 Dark cell, bread and water........	11 days
6 Dark cell, bread and water........	3 days	1 Dark cell, bread and water........	12 days
22 Dark cell, bread and water........	4 days	4 Dark cell, bread and water........	13 days
15 Dark cell, bread and water........	5 days	1 Dark cell, bread and water........	14 days
39 Dark cell. bread and water........	6 days	1 Dark cell. bread and water........	15 days
10 Dark cell, bread and water........	7 days	1 Dark cell, bread and water........	17 days
11 Dark cell, bread and water........	8 days	1 Dark cell, bread and water........	18 days
6 Dark cell, bread and water........	9 days	1 Dark cell, bread and water........	26 days
18 Dark cell, bread and wnter........	10 days	1 Dark cell, bread and water........	35 days

Total number of prisoners punished, 140.

TABLE NO. 13.

Showing the Number of Prisoners Confined in the State Prison Who Cannot Read, Cannot Write, Have Attended School One Year or Less, Six Months or Less, and Who Have Never Attended School.

Cannot read	21
Cannot write	25
Attended school one year or less	1
Attended school six months or less	15
Never attended school	28

TABLE NO. 14.

Showing the Term of Sentence of the Prisoners Above Described, viz: Those Who Cannot Read, Cannot Write, Etc.

1 year	5	6 years and 6 months	1
1 year and 6 months	5	8 years	4
2 years	5	9 years	1
2 years and 6 months	1	10 years	3
2 years and 9 months	1	14 years	1
3 years	3	30 years	1
4 years	2	Life	4
5 years	7		
6 years	1	Total	45

TABLE NO. 15.

Showing the Number of Prisoners in the State Prison Having Money to Their Credit Prior to December 1, 1891, and the amount. Number Receiving and Earning Money Since December 1, 1891, and the Amount. Number Expending Money While in Prison, and the Amount, and Number Having Money to their Credit at the End of the Year, and the Amount.

Number of prisoners having money December 1, 1891	69	$ 805 42
Total amount so held		
Number of prisoners receiving and earning money during the fiscal year ending December 1, 1892	157	
Amount so received and earned		6,683 04
Number of prisoners expending money during the fiscal year ending Dec. 1, 1892	155	
Total amount so expended		5,934 52
Number of prisoners having money to their credit on December 1, 1892	159	
Total amount so credited		1,553 94

TABLE NO 16.

Showing the Total Number of Prisoners Released From the State Prison by Expiration of Sentence, Pardon, Etc.

Discharged by expiration of sentence	123
Discharged by pardon	17
Discharged on writ of habeas corpus	1
Transferred to insane asylum	1
Died	3
Total number released	145

TABLE NO. 17.

Showing Length of "Good Time" Allowed Prisoners Discharged From the State Prison From Dec. 1, 1891, to Dec. 1, 1892.

1 Prisoner allowed 16 days good time
1 Prisoner allowed 22 days good time.
3 Prisoners allowed 24 days good time each
7 Prisoners allowed 28 days good days each.
44 Prisoners allowed 1 month good time each.
1 Prisoner allowed 1 month, 4 days good time.
1 Prisoner allowed 1 month, 5 days good time.
1 Prisoner allowed 1 month, 24 days good time.
4 Prisoners allowed 1 month, 28 days good time each.
6 Prisoners allowed 2 months good time each.
1 Prisoner allowed 2 months, 8 days good time.
1 Prisoner allowed 2 months, 24 days good time.
6 Prisoners allowed 2 months, 28 days good time each.
16 Prisoners allowed 3 months good time each.
1 Prisoner allowed 3 months, 3 days good time.
1 Prisoner allowed 4 months, 1 day good time.
1 Prisoner allowed 5 months, 24 days good time.
2 Prisoners allowed 5 months, 28 days good time each.
5 Prisoners allowed 6 months good time each.
3 Prisoners allowed 9 months, 28 days good time each.
1 Prisoner allowed 10 months good time.
1 Prisoner allowed 1 year, 2 months and 28 days good time.
4 Prisoners allowed 1 year, 3 months good time each.
3 Prisoners allowed 2 years, 3 months good time each.
1 Prisoner allowed 2 years, 6 months good time.
1 Prisoner allowed 2 years, 9 months good time.
1 Prisoner allowed 3 years, 8 months good time.
1 Prisoner allowed 3 years, 9 months good time.
1 Prisoner allowed 6 years, 3 months good time.

120 Prisoners allowed good time.
17 Prisoners pardoned.
3 Prisoners died.
5 Prisoners not allowed good time.

145 Prisoners released from the State Prison since December 1, 1891.

TABLE NO 18.

Showing the Number of Prisoners Furnished with Cash Gratuity when Discharged, and the Amount so Furnished.

Number of prisoners furnished cash gratuity......	130
Number of prisoners having sufficient money.....	15
Total number discharged	145
Total amount of money so furnished.....	$650

TABLE NO. 19.

Showing the Number of Prisoners Furnished with Clothing when Discharged, and the Value of the Clothing so Furnished.

Number of Prisoners furnished clothing	133
Number of prisoners having suitable clothing ..	12
Total number discharged.....	145
Total value of clothing so furnished	$1,830

TABLE NO. 20.

Showing the Number of Previous Commitments of the Prisoners now Confined in the State Prison.

No previous commitments	332
One previous commitment.....	9
Two previous commitments.....	1
Three previous commitments.....	1
Total.....	343

TABLE NO 21.

Showing Conduct of Prisoners in Prison for Fiscal Year ending Dec. 1, 1892, who were Discharged during said year.

Fair	13
Very good	98
Good	27
Bad	2
Very bad	4
Not given	1
Total discharged	145

TABLE NO. 22.

Showing the Number of Prisoners in the State Prison prior to Dec. 1, 1891; the Number Received and Released since said Date, and the Number in Prison at the Present Time.

Number in prison Dec. 1, 1891	308
Total number released	145
	163
Number received since Dec. 1, 1891	180
Total number in prison Dec. 1, 1892	343

TABLE NO. 23.

Showing the Number of Prisoners Confined in the Penitentiary at Deer Lodge, Montana, on the last Day of each Month, from July, 1872, to December 1st, 1892.

Month	1872 No. of Prisoners	1873 No. of Prisoners	1874 No. of Prisoners	1875 No. of Prisoners	1876 No. of Prisoners	1877 No. of Prisoners	1878 No. of Prisoners	1879 No. Prisoners	1880 No. of Prisoners	1881 No. of Prisoners	1882 No. of Prisoners	1883 No. of Prisoners	1884 No. of Prisoners	1885 No. of Prisoners	1886 No. of Prisoners	1887 No. of Prisoners	1888 No. of Prisoners	1889 No. of Prisoners	1890 No. of Prisoners	1891 No. of Prisoners	1892 No. of Prisoners
January	....	21	22	22	20	29	27	35	44	55	57	57	66	38	78	121	147	155	193	236	324
February	....	18	20	22	20	28	27	33	44	55	57	53	66	40	109	122	144	152	198	252	344
March	....	21	22	22	22	28	28	32	44	57	56	54	66	49	119	111	145	149	198	257	330
April	....	21	21	22	22	29	28	35	44	58	60	62	69	47	117	121	148	147	204	254	331
May	....	20	24	22	23	27	27	37	50	58	60	67	58	42	117	125	152	154	217	256	342
June	....	19	24	22	23	27	27	36	57	53	67	68	56	55	112	126	151	155	222	280	345
July	....	21	24	22	24	27	26	35	55	62	68	72	52	55	109	130	156	167	215	301	350
August	20	25	20	22	25	27	31	32	53	64	66	72	56	55	115	135	146	165	227	305	340
September	24	22	20	23	25	26	30	31	53	63	67	75	52	55	110	136	111	172	213	289	344
October	17	22	21	22	25	22	30	36	54	55	62	76	55	38	105	142	141	175	228	308	357
November	19	23	22	22	25	21	37	40	53	60	72	69	104	71	122	144	152	174	442	315	343
December	22	21	22	22	19	21	..	..	..	..	..	..	..	..	..	..	..	..	240	..	....

TABLE A.

Showing the Amount Paid Contractors Monthly for the Keeping of Convicts for the Fiscal Year, Commencing Dec. 1, 1891, and ending Dec. 1, 1892, and the Amount Paid Out Monthly for Clothing for Discharged Convicts, and the Amount of Money Paid Out to Such Convicts During Said Fiscal Year.

EXPENSE OF KEEPING CONVICTS.

From December 2, 1891, to December 20, 1891.

From December 2, 1891, to December 20, 1891, both inclusive, the State paid out for the care and keeping of convicts, as follows:

100 convicts 1,900 days at 70 cents per capita per day	$1,330 00
217 convicts 4,040 days at 65 cents per capita per day	2,626 00

317　　5,940　　$3,956 00

The State paid out for clothing and cash gratuity on December 20, 1891, for four convicts discharged between the 1st and 20th of December, 1891, as follows:

Clothing	$60 00
Cash gratuity	10 00
	70 00

Total expenses of State Prison for 19 days from December 2, 1891, to December 20, 1891 ... $4,026 00

EXPENSE OF KEEPING CONVICTS.

From December 21, 1891, to January 17, 1892.

From December 21, 1891, to January 17, 1892, the State paid out for the care and keeping of convicts as follows:

100 convicts 2,800 days at 70 cents per capita per day	$1,960 00
220 convicts 6,233 days at 65 cents per capita per day	4,051 45

320　　9,033　　$6,011 45

The State paid out for clothing and cash gratuity on January 18, 1892, for five convicts discharged between December 21, 1892, and January 17, 1891, as follows:

Clothing	$75 00
Cash gratuity	25 00
	100 00

Total expenses of State Prison for 28 days from December 21, 1891 to January 17, 1892 ... $6,111 45

EXPENSE OF KEEPING CONVICTS.

From January 18, 1892, to February 14, 1892.

From January 18, 1892, to February 14, 1892, the State paid out for the care and keeping of convicts as follows:

100 convicts 2,800 days at 70 cents per capita per day	$1,960 00
223 convicts 6,228 days at 65 cents per capita per day	4,047 55

323　　9,028　　$6,007 55

The State paid out for clothing and cash gratuity on February 15, 1892, for 10 convicts discharged between January 18, 1892, and February 14, 1892, as follows:

Clothing	$145 00
Cash gratuity	40 00
	185 00
For additional cells to Penitentiary	1,379 17

Total expense of State Prison for 28 days from January 18, 1892, to February 14, 1892 ... $7,571 72

EXPENSE OF KEEPING CONVICTS.

From February 15, 1892, to March 20, 1892.

From February 15, 1892, to March 20, 1892, both inclusive, the State paid out for the care and keeping of convicts, as follows:

100 convicts 3,500 days at 70 cents per capita per day	$2,450 00
225 convicts 7,778 days at 65 cents per capita per day	5,055 70

325   11,278

$7,505 70

The State paid out for clothing and cash gratuity on March 21, 1892, for 12 convicts discharged between February 15, 1892 and March 20, 1892, as follows:

Clothing	$180 00	
Cash gratuity	55 00	
		235 00

Total expense of State Prison for 35 days from February 15, 1892, to March 20, 1892.

$7,740 70

EXPENSE OF KEEPING CONVICTS.

From March 21, 1892, to April 17, 1892.

From March 21, 1892, to April 17, 1892, both inclusive, the State paid out for the care and keeping of convicts as follows:

100 convicts 2,800 days at 70 cents per capita per day	$1,960 00
227 convicts 6,438 days at 65 cents per capita per day	4,184 70

327   9,238

$6,144 70

The State paid out for clothing and cash gratuity on April 18, 1892, for nine convicts discharged between March 21, 1892, and April 17, 1892, as follows:

Clothing	$130 00	
Cash gratuity	40 00	
		170 00

Total expense of State Prison for 28 days from March 21, 1892, to April 17, 1892.

$6,314 70

EXPENSE OF KEEPING CONVICTS.

From April 18, 1892, to May 15, 1892.

From April 18, 1892, to May 15, 1892, both inclusive, the State paid out for the care and keeping of convicts as follows:

100 convicts 2,800 days at 70 cents per capita per day	$1,960 00
229 convicts 6,526 days at 65 cents per capita per day	4,241 90

329   9,326

$6,201 90

The State paid out for clothing and cash gratuity on May 14, 1892, for four convicts discharged between April 18, 1892 and May 15, 1892, as follows:

Clothing	$60 00	
Cash gratuity	20 00	
		80 00

Total expense of State Prison for 28 days from April 18, 1892, to May 15, 1892.

$6,281 00

EXPENSE OF KEEPING CONVICTS.

From May 16, 1892, to June 19, 1892.

From May 16, 1892, to June 19, 1892, both inclusive, the State paid out for the care and keeping of convicts as follows:

100 convicts 3,500 days at 70 cents per capita per day..	$2,450 00
234 convicts 8,349 days at 65 cents per capita per day..	5,426 85
334 11,849	$7,876 85

The State paid out for clothing and cash gratuity on June 20, 1892, for 18 convicts discharged between May 16, 1892, and June 19, 1892, as follows:

Clothing.. $236 00	
Cash gratuity... 70 00	
	306 00

Total expense of State Prison for 35 days from May 16, 1892, to June 19, 1892....	$8,182 85

EXPENSE OF KEEPING CONVICTS.

From June 20, 1892, to July 17, 1892.

From June 20, 1892, to July 17, 1892, both inclusive, the State paid out for the care and keeping of convicts as follows:

100 convicts 2,800 days at 70 cents per capita per day	$1,960 00
246 convicts 6,857 days at 65 cents per capita per day.................................	4,457 05
346 9,657	$6,417 05

The State paid out for clothing and cash gratuity on July 18, 1892, for 13 convicts discharged between June 20, 1892, and July 17, 1892, as follows:

Clothing $187 00	
Cash gratuity........... .... 60 00	
	247 00
For building hospital........	262 44

Total expense of State Prison for 28 days from June 20, 1892, to July 17, 1892.. ...	$6,926 49

EXPENSE OF KEEPING CONVICTS.

From July 18, 1892, to August 14, 1892.

From July 18, 1892, to August 14, 1892, both inclusive, the State paid out for the care and keeping of convicts as follows:

100 convicts 2,800 days at 70 cents per capita per day...............................	$1,960 00
246 convicts 6,970 days at 65 cents per capita per day...............................	4,529 85
346 9,770	$6,489 85

The State paid out for clothing and cash gratuity on August 15, 1892, for 12 convicts discharged between July 18, 1892, and August 14, 1892, as follows:

Clothing... $180 00	
Cash gratuity... 55 00	
	235 00

Total expense of State Prison for 28 days from July 18, 1892, to August 14, 1892....	$6,724 85

EXPENSE OF KEEPING CONVICTS.

From August 15, 1892, to September 18, 1892.

From August 5, 1892, to September 18, 1892, both inclusive, the State paid out for the care and keeping of convicts as follows:

100 convicts, 3,500 days at 70 cents per capita per day..............................	$2,450 00
235 convicts, 8,414 days at 65 cents per capita per day..............................	5,469 10
335 11,914	$7,919 19

The state State paid out for clothing and cash gratuity on September 19, 1892, for 16 convicts discharged between August 15, 1892, and September 18, 1892, as follows:

Clothing..	$199 00
Cash gratuity......	60 00
	259 00

Total expense of State Prison for 35 days, from August 15, 1892, to September 18, 1892... $8,178 10

EXPENSE OF KEEPING CONVICTS

From September 19, 1892, to October 16, 1892.

From September 19, 1892, to October 16, 1892, both inclusive, the State paid out for the care and keeping of convicts as follows:

100 convicts, 2,800 days at 70 cents per capita per day..................... .....$1,960 00	
260 convicts, 6,924 days at 65 cents per capita per day...... .... 4,500 60	
360 9,724	$6,460 60	$6,460 60

The State paid out for clothing and cash gratuity on October 17, 1892, for eight convicts discharged between September 19, 1892, and October 16, 1892, as follows:

Clothing............................... .. .. $97 00	
Cash gratuity 40 00	
	137 00

Total expense of State Prison for 28 days from September 19, 1892, to October 16, 1892... $6,460 60

The appropriation for the care and keeping of the convicts being exhausted, the bill for boarding the convicts was allowed in the sum above mentioned but not transmitted to the State Auditor.

EXPENSE OF KEEPING CONVICTS.

From October 17, 1892, to November 20, 1892.

From October 17, 1892, to November 20, 1892, both inclusive, the State paid out for the care and keeping of convicts as follows:

100 convicts, 3,500 days at 70 cents per capita per day................................	$2,450 00
242 convicts, 8,788 days at 65 cents per capita per day....	5,712 20
342 12,288	$8,162 20

The State paid out for clothing and cash gratuity on Nov. 21, 1892, for 23 convicts discharged between October 17, 1892, and November 20, 1892, as follows:

Clothing.. $291 00	
Cash gratuity.. 115 00	
	406 00

Total expense of State Prison for 35 days from October 17, 1892, to November 20, 1892 .... $8,568 20

The appropriation for the care and keeping of the convicts being exhausted, the bill for boarding the convicts was allowed in the sum above mentioned, but not transmitted to the State Auditor.

EXPENSE OF KEEPING CONVICTS

From November 21, 1892, to November 30, 1892.

From November 21, 1892, to November 30, 1892, both inclusive the State paid out for the care and keeping of convicts as follows:

100 convicts, 1 000 days at 70 cents per capita per day.....................................	$ 700 00
243 convicts, 2,130 days at 65 cents per capita per day.............	1,579 50
343 3,130	$2,279 50

The State paid out for clothing and cash gratuity on December 1, 1892, for three convicts discharged between November 21, 1892, and November 30, 1892, as follows:

Clothing............. .... $45 00	
Cash gratuity... 15 00	
	60 00

Total expense of State Prison for 10 days from November 21, 1892, to November 30, 1892............. .... $2,339 50

The appropriation for the keeping and care of the convicts being exhausted, the bill for boarding the convicts was allowed in the sum above mentioned, but not transmitted to the State Auditor.

Total expense of State Prison for 19 days, from December 2, 1891, to December 20, 1891	$ 4,026 00
Total expense of State Prison for 28 days, from December 21, 1891, to January 17, 1892..	6,111 45
Total expense of State Prison for 28 days, from January 18, 1892 to February 14, 1892...	7,571 72
Total expense of State Prison for 35 days, from February 15, 1892, to March 20, 1892....	7,740 70
Total expense of State Prison for 28 days, from March 21, 1892, to April 17, 1892........	6,314 70
Total expense of State Prison for 28 days from April 18, 1892, to May 15, 1892..........	6,281 90
Total expense of State Prison for 35 days, from May 16, 1892, to June 19, 1892.........	8,183 85
Total expense of State Prison for 28 days, from June 20, 1892, to July 17, 1892......... .	6,926 49
Total expense of State Prison for 28 days, from July 18, 1892, to August 14, 1892........	6,724 85
Total expense of State Prison for 35 days, from August 15, 1892 to September 18, 1892..	8,178 10
Total expense of State Prison for 28 days, from September 19, 1892, to October 16, 1892.	6,460 60
Total expense of State Prison for 35 days, from October 17, 1892 to November 20, 1892.	8,568 20
Total expense of State Prison for 10 days, from November 21, 1892, to November 30, 1892	2,339 50
Total..	$85,427 06

TABLE B.

Showing the Name of the Sheriff of Each County, County Wherein Prisoner Was Sentenced, Date of Admission to the Prison, Mileage Allowed Sheriff for Transporting Each Convict and the Amount Allowed, Mileage Allowed Sheriff to and From the Prison and the Amount Allowed, Total Number of Prisoners Taken From Each County and the Total Amount Allowed Each Sheriff for the Fiscal Year Ending December 1, 1892.

Name of Sheriff.	County Where Sentenced.	Date of Admission at the Prison.	Mileage Allowed for Transporting Convict	Amount Allowed Sheriff for Transporting Convict.	Mileage Allowed Sheriff to and From the State Prison.	Amount Allowed Sheriff for Miles to and From the State Prison.	Total Amount Allowed Sheriff for Transporting Convict.
A. O. Rose	Beaverhead	Dec. 28, 1892	113	$22 60	226	$22 60	$45 20
"	"	March 10, 1892	103	20 60	206	30 90	51 50
"	"	April 2, 1892	103	20 60	206	30 90	51 50
"	"	July 1, 1892	103	20 60	206	30 90	51 50
"	"	July 1, 1892	103	20 60			20 60
"	"	June 5, 1892	103	20 60	206	30 90	51 50
"	"	Sept. 21, 1892	103	20 60	206	30 90	51 50
"	"	Sept. 20, 1892	103	20 60	206	30 90	51 50
"	"	Nov. 18, 1892	103	20 60			20 60
				30 90	206	30 90	20 00
Total		No. admitted 10		$108 00		$238 90	$446 90
Josephus Hamilton	Cascade	De 6, 1891	161	$32 20	322	$48 30	$80 50
"	"	Dec. 12, 1890	161	32 20	322	48 30	80 50
"	"	Dec. 18, 1891	161	32 20	322	48 30	80 50
"	"	Dec. 20, 1891	161	32 20	322	48 30	80 50
"	"	Dec. 23, 1891	161	32 20	322	48 30	80 50
"	"	Dec. 28, 1891	161	32 20	322	48 30	80 50
"	"	Jan. 22, 1892	162	32 40	324	48 60	81 00
"	"	June 23, 1892	162	32 40	324	48 60	81 00
"	"	June 24, 1892	162	32 40	324	48 60	81 00
Total		No. admitted 9		$290 40		$435 60	$726 00
B. F. O'Neal	Choteau	Dec. 12, 1891	207	$41 40	414	$62 10	$103 50
"	"	Dec. 15, 1891	207	41 40	414	62 10	103 50

$103 50 $88 88 88 88 88 88 88 88 88 88 88 41 50 41 50 41 50	$62 10 61 61 61 61 61 62 61 61 62 62 62 10 62 10 62 79	44 50 41 41 41 41 41 41 41 41 41 41 41 41 41 41	$41 50 41 41 41 41 41 41 41 41 41 41 41 41 41 41	207 200 200 200 200 200 207 200 200 207 207 207 207 207 207	Dec. 18, 1891 Mar. 12, 1892 Mar. 14, 1892 Mar. 15, 1892 Mar. 19, 1892 Mar. 4, 1892 May 30, 1892 May 31, 1892 June 5, 1892 July 20, 1892 July 30, 1892 Sept. 30, 1892 Oct. 1, 1892 Oct. 3, 1892	H. F. O'Neil ... Choteau ...

No. admitted 20

| $1,941 30 | $1,115 10 | | $826 20 | | | Total ... |

| $213 00 112 112 112 112 112 | $127 00 127 127 127 127 127 | $50 00 $50 $50 $50 $50 $50 | $50 00 88 88 88 88 88 | 124 125 125 125 125 125 | Dec. 31, 1891 May 25, 1892 July 18, 1892 Sept. 20, 1892 Sept. 21, 1892 Sept. 25, 1892 | Ed. J. Jones ... Custer ... |

No. admitted 6

| $1,274 50 | $764 70 | | $599 50 | | | Total ... |

| $7 00 | | | $7 00 | | Nov. 19, 1892 July 20, 1892 July 30, 1892 Aug. 3, 1892 Aug. 3, 1892 July 2, 1892 July 25, 1892 June 13, 1892 May 7, 1892 Mar. 21, 1892 Mar. 15, 1892 Feb. 16, 1862 | James T. Quigley ... Deer Lodge ... |

No. admitted 11

| | | | | | | Total ... |

TABLE B.—CONTINUED.

NAME OF SHERIFF.	County Where Sentenced.	Date of Admission at the Prison.	Mileage Allowed for Transporting Convict.	Amount Allowed Sheriff for Transporting Convict.	Mileage Allowed to Sheriff to and from the State Prison.	Amount Allowed Sheriff for Mileage to and from the State Prison.	Total Amount Allowed Sheriff for Transporting Convict.
Joel Gleason	Dawson						
Maurice Sullivan	Fergus	April 4, 1892	291	$55 20	582	$87 30	$145 50
"	"	June 24, 1892	191	68 80	583	118 50	217 80
"	"	June 24, 1892	491	68 80			68 80
"	"	Sept. 8, 1892	291	55 20	582	55 30	115 50
"	"	Sept. 9, 1892	291	55 20	582	57 30	145 50
Total		No. admitted 5		$372 20		$110 10	$782 30
James M. Robertson	Gallatin	Sept. 21, 1892	138	$27 80	278	$41 70	$69 50
Dodley Halford	Jefferson	Feb. 14, 1892	78	15 60	150	23 40	39 00
"	"	Dec. 14, 1891	78	16 00	150	24 00	40 00
"	"	July 20, 1892	78	15 60	156	23 40	39 00
"	"	Oct. 10, 1892	78	15 60	156	23 40	39 00
Total		No. admitted 4		$62 80		$94 20	$157 00
Charles M. Jeffries	Lewis and Clarke	Dec. 5, 1891	65	13 00	130	$19 50	$32 50
"	"	Jan. 3, 1892	65	13 00	130	19 50	32 50
"	"	Jan. 17, 1892	65	13 00	130	19 50	32 50
"	"	Jan. 19, 1892	65	13 00	130	18 90	31 90
"	"	Mar. 15, 1892	63	12 60	126	18 90	31 50
"	"	Mar. 29, 1892	63	12 60	126	18 90	31 50
"	"	Mar. 30, 1892	63	12 60	126	18 90	31 50
"	"	April 9, 1892	63	12 60	126	18 90	31 50
"	"	May 11, 1892	63	12 60	126	18 90	31 50
"	"	July 1, 1892	63	12 60	126	18 90	31 50
"	"	July 2, 1892	63	12 60	126	18 90	31 50
"	"	Nov. 22, 1892	63	12 60	126	18 90	31 50
"	"	July 3, 1892	63	12 60	126	18 90	31 50
"	"	July 4, 1892	63	12 60	126	18 90	31 50
"	"	July 23, 1892	63	12 60	126	18 90	31 50
"	"	July 24, 1892	63	12 60	126	18 90	31 50

Name	County	Date	Admitted					
Charles M. Jeffries	Lewis and Clarke	June 29, 1892	63	$12 60	126	$18 90	$31 50	
"		June 30, 1892	63	12 60	126	18 90	31 50	
"		Sept. 23, 1892	63	12 60	126	18 90	31 50	
"		Sept. 24, 1892	63	12 60	126	18 90	31 50	
Total		No. admitted 20		$253 60		$380 40	$634 00	
Mark Brown	Madison	May 9, 1892	136	$27 20	272	$40 80	$68 00	
Charles T. Rader	Meagher	May 9, 1892	136	27 20	272	40 80	68 00	
"		Sept. 30, 1892	136	27 20	272	40 80	68 00	
Total		No. admitted 3		$81 60		$122 40	$204 00	
W. H. Houston	Missoula	Mar. 23, 1892	96	$17 20	172	$25 80	$43 00	
"		Mar. 24, 1892	86	17 20	172	25 80	43 00	
"		Mar. 25, 1892	88	17 20	172	25 80	43 00	
"		Mar. 28, 1892	86	17 20	172	25 80	43 00	
"		April 22, 1892	86	17 20	172	25 80	43 00	
"		May 4, 1892	86	17 20	172	25 80	43 00	
"		May 5, 1892	86	17 20	172	25 80	43 00	
"		May 6, 1892	90	18 00	180	27 00	45 00	
"		Dec. 21, 1891	90	18 00	176	27 00	45 00	
"		Dec. 31, 1892	95	17 00	176	26 40	44 00	
"		Aug. 1, 1892	95	17 00	176	26 40	44 00	
"		Sept. 9, 1892	95	17 00	176	26 40	44 00	
"		Sept. 20, 1892	95	17 00	176	26 40	44 00	
"		Sept. 21, 1892	95	17 00	176	26 40	44 00	
"		Oct. 15, 1892	95	17 00	176	26 40	44 00	
"		Oct. 21, 1893	88	17 00	176	26 40	44 00	
Total		No. admitted 17		$296 80		$445 20	$742 00	
O. P. Templeton	Park	Feb. 25, 1892	161	$32 20	322	$48 30	$80 50	
"		Feb. 27, 1892	161	32 20	322	48 30	80 50	
"		Feb. 24, 1892	171	32 20	322	48 30	80 50	
"		April 25, 1892	161	32 20	322	48 30	80 50	
"		April 28, 1892	161	32 20	322	48 30	80 50	
"		Aug. 5, 1892	100	32 00	320	48 00	80 00	
"		Nov. 20, 1892	100	32 00	320	48 00	80 00	
Total		No. admitted 7		$225 00		$337 50	$562 50	

TABLE B—Concluded.

Name of Sheriff.	County Where Sentenced.	Date of Admission at the Prison.	Mileage Allowed for Transporting Convict.	Amount Allowed Sheriff for Transporting Convict.	Mileage Allowed to Sheriff to and from the State Prison.	Amount Allowed Sheriff for Mileage to and from State Prison.	Total Amount Allowed Sheriff for Each Convict.
John E. Lloyd	Silver Bow	Dec. 5, 1891	42	$8 40	84	$12 60	21 00
"	"	Dec. 6, 1891	42	8 40	84	12 60	31 00
"	"	Dec. 13, 1891	42	8 40	84	12 60	21 00
"	"	Dec. 14, 1891	42	8 40	84	12 60	21 00
"	"	Dec. 20, 1891	42	8 40	84	12 60	21 00
"	"	Dec. 28, 1891	42	8 40	84	12 60	21 00
"	"	Dec. 31, 1891	42	8 40	84	12 60	21 00
"	"	Jan. 28, 1892	42	8 40			8 40
"	"	Jan. 28, 1892	42	8 40			8 40
"	"	Jan. 28, 1892	42	8 40			8 40
"	"	Jan. 28, 1892	42	8 40			8 40
"	"	Jan. 28, 1892	42	8 40			8 40
"	"	Feb. 17, 1892	42	8 40	84	12 60	30 00
"	"	Feb. 20, 1892	42	8 40	84	12 60	21 00
"	"	Feb. 28, 1892	42	8 40	84	12 60	21 00
"	"	Mar. 7, 1892	42	8 40	84	12 60	21 00
"	"	Mar. 13, 1892	42	8 40	84	12 60	41 00
"	"	April 27, 1892	42	8 40	84	12 60	21 00
"	"	May 1, 1892	42	8 40			8 40
"	"	May 1, 1892	42	8 40			8 40
"	"	May 8, 1892	42	8 40	84	12 60	21 00
"	"	May 15, 1892	42	8 40	84	12 60	21 00
"	"	Oct. 31, 1892	42	8 40	84	12 60	21 00
"	"	May 11, 1892	42	8 40	84	12 60	21 00
"	"	May 30, 1892	42	8 40	84	12 60	21 00
"	"	June 18, 1892	42	8 40	84	12 60	21 00
"	"	June 18, 1892	42	8 40	84	12 60	21 00
"	"	June 19, 1892	42	8 40	84	12 60	21 00
"	"	June 19, 1892	42	8 40	84	12 60	21 00
"	"	June 23, 1892	42	8 40	84	12 60	21 00
"	"	June 23, 1892	42	8 40	84	12 60	21 00

Sheriff was allowed $8 per day for deputies and made no charge for mileage, as appears above.

John E. Lloyd

Name	County	Date admitted	No.	Amount	Miles	Amount	Total
John E. Lloyd	Silver Bow	June 26, 1892	42	$8 40	84	$12 00	$11 00
"	"	June 26, 1892	42	$8 40	84	12 00	21 00
"	"	June 27, 1892	42	8 40	84	12 00	21 00
"	"	June 27, 1892	42	8 40	84	12 00	21 00
"	"	June 28, 1892	42	8 40	84	12 00	21 00
"	"	June 29, 1892	42	8 40	84	12 00	21 00
"	"	June 29, 1892	42	8 40	84	12 00	21 00
"	"	July 9, 1892	42	8 40	84	12 00	21 00
"	"	Sept. 2, 1892	42	8 40	84	12 00	21 00
"	"	Sept. 26, 1892	42	8 40	84	12 00	21 00
"	"	Oct. 5, 1892	42	8 40	84	12 00	21 00
"	"	Oct. 5, 1892	42	8 40	84	12 00	21 00
"	"	Oct. 9, 1892	42	8 40	84	12 00	21 00
"	"	Oct. 9, 1892	42	8 40	84	12 00	21 00
"	"	Oct. 9, 1892	42	8 40	84	12 00	21 00
"	"	Oct. 9, 1892	42	8 40	84	12 00	21 00
"	"	Oct. 9, 1892	42	8 40	84	12 00	21 00
"	"	Oct. 9, 1892	42	8 40	84	12 00	21 00
"	"	Nov. 21, 1892	42	8 40	84	12 00	21 00
"	"	Nov. 29, 1892	42	8 40	84	12 00	21 00
"	"	Oct. 7, 1892	42	8 40	84	12 00	21 00
"	"	Oct. 9, 1892	42	8 40	84	12 00	21 00
Total			No. admitted 10	$594 00		$607 80	$1,201 80
John M. Ramsey	Yellowstone	May 27, 1892	277	$55 40	554	$83 10	$138 50
"	"	May 25, 1892	277	55 40	554	83 10	138 50
"	"	Oct. 10, 1892	297	59 40	591	89 10	148 50
"	"	Oct. 10, 1892	297	59 40	594	89 10	148 50
Total			No. admitted 4	$229 60		$344 40	$574 00

(1.) The extra expense for transporting this prisoner was occasioned by the wash-outs, which compelled the Sheriff to go to Deer Lodge by way of Logan, thereby making an additional travel of 100 miles.

(2.) At the time the last two prisoners were transported to Deer Lodge a bridge on the Logan and Butte branch of the Northern Pacific & Montana was burned out, which necessitated the taking these prisoners by the way of Helena, which accounts for the extra mileage.

Number of prisoners admitted to State Prison during the fiscal year ending December 1, 1892..... 180
Total amount allowed sheriffs for transporting convicts for said fiscal year..... $3,847 00
Total amount allowed sheriffs for mileage to and from State Prison for said fiscal year..... 5,356 30
Allowed for extra deputies in Silver Bow County..... 30 00

Total amount allowed for transportation of convicts and mileage for sheriffs to and from State Prison for said fiscal year..... $9,253 30

TABLE C.

Showing the Office Expenses Incurred by the State Board of Prison Commissioners During the Fiscal Year Ending Dec. 1, 1892.

NAME OF PERSON RENDERING SERVICES OR FURNISHING SUPPLIES.	When incurred or Purchased.	Character of Service Rendered or Article for Which Expense was Incurred.	Amount Allowed and Paid.	Date When Paid.	Appropriation Paid From.
	1892.			1892.	
Independent Publishing Co.	Feb. 16	500 Letter heads	$ 1 50	Feb. 16	Public printing account
Independent Publishing Co.	Feb. 16	500 No. 6 Envelopes 2 cent stamp	11 50	Feb. 16	Public printing account
Alice Edmonson, clerk	Feb. 28	Services rendered Board of Prison Commissioners under direction of the Attorney General	100 00	Mar. 2	Traveling and office expense account of State Board Prison Commissioners
May Cuthbert, clerk	Feb. 28	Services rendered Board of Prison Commissioners under direction of the Attorney General	100 00	Mar. 2	Traveling and office expense account of State Board Prison Commissioners
J. B. Sanford	May 6	1 Rolled top desk	150 00	May 14	State officer's supply account
C. K. Wells & Co.	May 13	1 Index book	1 25	May 17	State officer's supply account
May Cuthbert, clerk	Sep. 30	Services rendered Board of Prison Commissioners under direction of the Attorney General	100 00	Sept. 30	Traveling and office expense account of State Board Prison Commissioners
May Miller	Sept. 30	Services rendered in office of Attorney General	110 00	Sept. 30	Traveling and office expense account of State Board Prison Commissioners
May Miller	Nov. 30	Services rendered Board of Prison Commissioners under direction of the Attorney General	110 00	Nov. 30	Expense account of Board of Pardons

www.ingramcontent.com/pod-product-compliance
Lightning Source LLC
Chambersburg PA
CBHW021634270326
41931CB00008B/1011